# THE CASTLES & PALACES OF THE
# TUDORS & STUARTS

## THE GOLDEN AGE OF BRITAIN'S HISTORIC & STATELY HOUSES

# THE CASTLES & PALACES OF THE
# TUDORS & STUARTS

## THE GOLDEN AGE OF BRITAIN'S HISTORIC & STATELY HOUSES

### CHARLES PHILLIPS

CONSULTANT: PROFESSOR RICHARD G WILSON FRHistS

southwater

This edition is published
by Southwater,
an imprint of Anness Publishing Ltd
Hermes House
88–89 Blackfriars Road
London SE1 8HA
tel. 020 7401 2077
fax 020 7633 9499
www.southwaterbooks.com;
www.annesspublishing.com

Anness Publishing has a new picture
agency outlet for images for publishing,
promotions or advertising. Please visit
our website www.practicalpictures.com
for more information.

UK agent: The Manning Partnership Ltd;
tel. 01225 478444; fax 01225 478440;
sales@manning-partnership.co.uk

UK distributor: Book Trade Services; tel.
0116 2759086; fax 0116 2759090;
uksales@booktradeservices.com;
exportsales@booktradeservices.com

North American agent/distributor:
National Book Network;
tel. 301 459 3366; fax 301 429 5746;
www.nbnbooks.com

Australian agent/distributor:
Pan Macmillan Australia; tel. 1300 135
113; fax 1300 135 103;
customer.service@macmillan.com.au

New Zealand agent/distributor:
David Bateman Ltd; tel. (09) 415 7664;
fax (09) 415 8892

Publisher: Joanna Lorenz
Editor: Joy Wotton
Designer: Nigel Partridge
Illustrators: Anthony Duke, Rob Highton
and Vanessa Card

## ETHICAL TRADING POLICY

At Anness Publishing we believe that
business should be conducted in an ethical
and ecologically sustainable way, with
respect for the environment and a proper
regard to the replacement of the natural
resources we employ.

As a publisher, we use a lot of wood pulp
to make high-quality paper for printing,
and that wood commonly comes from
spruce trees. We are therefore currently
growing more than 750,000 trees in three
Scottish forest plantations: Berrymoss (130
hectares/320 acres), West Touxhill (125
hectares/305 acres) and Deveron Forest (75
hectares/185 acres). The forests we manage
contain more than 3.5 times the number of
trees employed each year in making paper
for the books we manufacture.

Because of this ongoing ecological
investment programme, you, as our customer,
can have the pleasure and reassurance of
knowing that a tree is being cultivated on
your behalf to naturally replace the materials
used to make the book you are holding.

Our forestry programme is run in
accordance with the UK Woodland
Assurance Scheme (UKWAS) and will be
certified by the internationally recognized
Forest Stewardship Council (FSC). The FSC
is a non-government organization dedicated
to promoting responsible management of
the world's forests. Certification ensures
forests are managed in an environmentally
sustainable and socially responsible way. For
further information about this scheme, go to
www.annesspublishing.com/trees

## PUBLISHER'S NOTE

Although the advice and information in
this book are believed to be accurate and
true at the time of going to press, neither
the authors nor the publisher can accept
any legal responsiblity or liability for any
errors or omissions that may be made.

Previously published as part of a larger
volume, *The Complete Illustrated Guide to
the Castles, Palaces & Stately Houses of
Britain and Ireland*

*Page 1*: Marlborough House.
*Page 2*: Castle Howard.
*Page 3*: Hampton Court.
*Page 4 left to right*: Hampton Court,
Ingatestone Hall, Wakehurst Place.
*Page 5 left to right*: Leith Hall, Kingston
Lacy, Nottingham Castle.

# CONTENTS

# INTRODUCTION

The Tudor and Stuart monarchs were among the greatest royal builders in British history. James IV and James V of Scots created Holyrood Palace, Falkland Palace and Stirling Castle, introducing the French-Italian Renaissance style into Scotland. In England, Henry VII and Henry VIII, the first Tudor kings, were equally lavish, creating Richmond Palace, Hampton Court Palace and St James's Palace. The reign of Henry VIII's daughter Elizabeth I was also an extraordinarily rich period for architecture, with the construction of 'prodigy houses' such as Burghley House and Longleat House. With the establishment of the House of Stuart, under James I and Charles I, the great Inigo Jones – builder of the gracious Queen's House, Greenwich, and the elegant Banqueting Hall, Whitehall – pioneered classical architecture in England.

*Left: James V's Renaissance-style building at Holyrood Palace was designed for his first wife, Madeleine de Valois, but she died before she could enjoy it.*

# TUDOR AND STUART MANSIONS

The Tudor age brought about social changes in England and Wales as profound as those that followed the Norman Conquest of 1066. The accession of Henry Tudor as Henry VII in 1485 ended the long Wars of the Roses: as the heroic age of warrior lords and knights drew to a close, a new elite class of merchants and statesmen arose to take their place. Then, *c.*1536–41, as Supreme Head of the Church of England, Henry seized the lands and assets of the country's religious houses, including around a quarter of England's agricultural land, in the Dissolution of the Monasteries. To raise money, he sold much of it to the merchants and political operators of the new Tudor gentry, resulting in an unprecedentedly extensive and swift change of land ownership in England.

### A NEW LEVEL OF COMFORT

Great new country houses were built by these men, houses constructed and decorated by the masons and craftsmen who had previously worked for the Church. Initially, many lords continued to raise battlements and gatehouses, but increasingly, also, they fitted their houses with large glass windows – a sign that they did not fear attack.

By 1540, Henry VII and Henry VIII had between them reigned for more than 50 years. Although there were continuing fears of foreign invasion, particularly since the establishment of the Church of England had inspired a Franco-Spanish Roman Catholic alliance, the Tudors had resoundingly succeeded in delivering the domestic peace they promised the people following the Wars of the Roses.

The new Tudor country houses offered far greater comfort: the windows let in more light and the fitting of flues led to the introduction of coal-burning fireplaces and chimneys. The houses also began to provide more private living space for their owners. The Great Hall

*Above: Henry VIII's arms are carved upon the west front of Hampton Court.*

began to be neglected in favour of the warm 'solar' room and other private chambers on the first floor of the house.

### TUDOR PALACES

The early Tudor decades were also a time of lavish palace building. Henry VII replaced his fire-ravaged palace at Sheen in Surrey with the vast and ornate Richmond Palace, laid out over 10 acres (4ha) around wide courtyards and with a magnificent timber-roofed Great Hall 100ft (30m) in length. He also built a new palace at Greenwich, where Henry VIII was born in 1491, and developed Baynard's Castle from a Norman fortification in London.

Henry VIII created magnificent royal residences at Whitehall and Hampton Court out of houses seized from Cardinal Wolsey; he took possession of great episcopal palaces such as Hatfield House in Hertfordshire and Knole in Kent; he built many new houses, for example at Bridewell in London and Beaulieu in Essex; and he established the extravagantly splendid new palaces of

*Left: Burghley House, the largest and finest mansion of the first Elizabethan age.*

*Above: Scottish architect Sir William Bruce transformed Holyrood in the 1670s.*

St James's in London, Oatlands at Weybridge and Nonesuch near Ewell (both in Surrey). By his death in 1547, Henry possessed more than 40 palaces and houses – more than any other English monarch.

### PRODIGY HOUSES

Edward VI, Mary and Elizabeth I added nothing to the collection of royal palaces, beyond minor additions and necessary maintenance under Elizabeth. But although no new royal buildings were erected, the 45-year reign of Elizabeth saw the construction of a series of astonishingly grand country houses built in her honour. Burghley House in Linconshire, Longleat in Wiltshire, Holdenby in Northamptonshire, Wollaton Hall in Nottinghamshire and Loseley House in Surrey were all 'prodigy houses', built by leading courtiers competing to create a country estate worthy of the monarch revered as England's greatest treasure, and fit to receive her on one of her annual 'summer progresses' around England.

The desire to create a country house grand enough to receive a monarch also inspired lords in the reign of James I,

when Robert Cecil, 1st Earl of Salisbury, built Hatfield House in Hertfordshire and Thomas Howard, 1st Earl of Suffolk, built Audley End, Essex. Like Knole in Kent, Hatfield was originally an ecclesiastical palace and then one of Henry VIII's many grand residences, before it was transformed into the country seat of England's leading political family. Mary I and Elizabeth I spent much of their childhood at Hatfield, and Elizabeth received the news there that she was queen.

### CLASSICAL ARCHITECTURE

The era of James I and Charles I saw the rise of Inigo Jones, one of the greatest English architects. With the creation of the Queen's House in Greenwich, the Banqueting House in Whitehall a nd Wilton House in Wiltshire, Jones became the pioneer in England of 'classical' building inspired by both ancient Roman and Italian Renaissance architecture, and particularly by the writing and designs of Andrea Palladio. Jones's elegant buildings were a major influence on future generations of patrons and architects – especially on the members of the 18th-century Palladian movement, who drew their inspiration from the works of Palladio.

*Below: Montacute in Somerset was built in the 1590s of lovely honey-coloured stone.*

# ENGLAND TIMELINE

Above: One of the three sunken gardens at Hampton Court Palace.

Above: Burghley House, one of the 'prodigy houses' built in the reign of Elizabeth I.

Above: Marlborough House was the London home of the 1st Duke of Marlborough.

### 1485–1579

 *c.*1485 Cardinal John Morton, Bishop of Ely, builds the episcopal palace of Hatfield House, Hertfordshire.

1514–19 Cardinal Wolsey, Lord Chancellor, builds a magnificent Renaissance residence at Hampton Court Palace.

1537–41 James V remodels Falkland Palace to create Scotland's first palace in the continental Renaissance style.

*c.*1540 Lawrence Washington, ancestor of the first US President, George Washington, builds Sulgrave Manor in Northamptonshire on the site of the dissolved Priory of St Andrew.

*c.*1540 Henry VIII builds Deal Castle in Kent.

1540–45 Henry VIII builds Pendennis Castle near Falmouth in Cornwall.

1547–52 Edward, Duke of Somerset, builds the splendid Syon House in Middlesex.

1555 Sir William Cecil begins building Burghley House in Northamptonshire.

*c.*1565–75 Robert Dudley, Earl of Leicester, carries out grand rebuilding at Kenilworth Castle in Warwickshire.

1562 Sir William More begins the transformation of Loseley House in Surrey into a 'prodigy house'.

1567 Sir John Thynne begins building his great 'prodigy house' of Longleat House in Wiltshire.

### 1580–1629

 1580–88 Sir Francis Willoughby builds Wollaton Hall in Nottinghamshire.

*c.*1590 Sir Edward Phelips begins building Montacute House in Somerset.

1587 Work on Burghley House, Lincolnshire, completed, for Sir William Cecil, 1st Baron Burghley.

1591–97 Elizabeth, Countess of Shrewsbury – 'Bess of Hardwick' – builds Hardwick Hall in Derbyshire.

1603–08 Thomas Sackville, 1st Earl of Dorset, rebuilds the elegant country house of Knole in Kent.

1605–14 Thomas Howard, 1st Earl of Suffolk, builds Audley End in Essex.

1607–08 Robert Cecil, 1st Earl of Salisbury, rebuilds Hatfield House in Hertfordshire.

1612 The leading Elizabethan 'surveyor' (architect), Robert Smythson, begins work at Bolsover Castle in Chesterfield, his last major house.

1615 Inigo Jones begins work on the Queen's House, Greenwich, based on an Italian Medici villa at Poggio a Caiano.

1616–25 Robert Lyminge builds Blickling Hall in Norfolk for Sir Henry Hobart.

1619–22 Inigo Jones builds the Banqueting House in Whitehall Palace.

1623 Inigo Jones begins work on the Queen's Chapel in St James's Palace.

### 1630–1714

 1636–40 Major work by Philip Herbert, 4th Earl of Pembroke, at his Wilton House in Wiltshire includes a new south front designed by Isaac de Caus and Inigo Jones.

*c.*1675 Charles II spends £130,000 at Windsor Castle, building new state apartments, and redecorating St George's Hall and the King's Chapel.

1687–1707 William Cavendish, 4th Earl of Devonshire, entirely rebuilds Chatsworth House in Derbyshire.

1688–96 Charles Seymour, 6th Duke of Somerset, builds Petworth House on the site of a 13th-century castle in West Sussex.

1689 Sir Christopher Wren begins rebuilding Hampton Court Palace for King William III and Queen Mary II. In the same year rebuilding begins to transform Nottingham House, Kensington, into Kensington Palace.

*c.*1690 Ford, Lord Grey of Werke, builds Uppark, West Sussex.

1696–1702 Nicholas Hawksmoor designs Easton Neston in Northamptonshire, regarded by some as the first country house in the Baroque style.

1709–11 Sir Christopher Wren builds Marlborough House in London for John Churchill, 1st Duke of Marlborough, and his wife, Sarah, Duchess of Marlborough.

N

W · E

S

SCOTLAND

North Sea

Irish Sea

Belsay Hall

ENGLAND

Bolsover Castle

Chatsworth

Hardwicke Hall & Old Hall

Wollaton Hall

Belton House

The Wash

Felbrigg Hall

Blickling Hall

Caister Castle

Burghley House

Boughton House

Kenilworth Castle

Audley End House

Woburn Abbey

Sulgrave Manor

Tower of London

WALES

The Banqueting House, Palace of Westminster

Hatfield House

Mapledurham House

Syon House

Queen's House

Windsor Castle

Eltham Palace

Deal Castle

Bristol Channel

Longleat

Hampton Court Palace

Hever Castle

Knole

Walmer Castle

Loseley Park

Strait of Dover

Winchester Castle Great Hall

Goodwood House

Montacute House

Anthony House

Portland Castle

St Mawes Castle

Pendennis Castle

English Channel

*Above: Holyrood Palace is the official residence in Scotland of the Queen.*

### SCOTLAND

**1512** James IV of Scots builds a Great Tower at Rothesay Castle, Isle of Bute.

*c.*1530 George Gordon, 4th Earl of Huntly, begins major rebuilding of Huntly Castle, Aberdeenshire.

**1536** James V of Scots completes major rebuilding of Holyrood Palace.

**1537–41** James V's rebuilding at Falkland Palace creates Scotland's first Renaissance palace.

**1538–42** James V builds a palace within Stirling Castle.

*c.*1580 Lord Edzell builds a courtyard mansion at Edzell Castle, Angus.

*c.*1585 5th Earl of Bothwell rebuilds Crichton Castle in the Renaissance style.

**1594** The construction of Crathes Castle in Aberdeenshire is completed.

*c.*1595 9th Lord Glamis embarks on a remodelling of Glamis Castle, Angus.

*c.*1600 King James VI of Scots builds Dunfermline Palace.

**1626** William Forbes completes Craigievar Castle in Aberdeenshire.

*c.*1675 Charles II rebuilds Holyrood Palace in Edinburgh.

**1628** John Erskine, 3rd Earl of Mar, builds Braemar Castle, Aberdeenshire.

**1640** Threave Castle, Dumfries and Galloway, surrenders after a 13-week siege.

**1699** The decay of Tantallon Castle, E Lothian, begins when the Douglas earls of Angus sell it.

**N**
**W** **E**
**S**

**North Sea**

**Moray Firth**

Huntly Castle

Castle Fraser

Crathes Castle

Braemar Castle

Glamis Castle    Edzell Castle

**S C O T L A N D**

Stirling Castle    Falkland Palace

**Firth of Forth**

Dunfermline Abbey & Palace

Linlithgow Palace    Tantallon Castle

Crichton Castle

Edinburgh Castle, Holyroodhouse Palace

**North Atlantic Ocean**

Threave Castle

**Solway Firth**

**E N G L A N D**

**Irish Sea**

Irish Sea

Flint Castle

Plas Mawr

Bryn Bras Castle

Bachecraig

Chirk Castle

Powis Castle

ENGLAND

Cardigan Bay

WALES

Carew Castle

Laugharne Castle

Bristol Channel

*Above: Carew Castle stands on the tidal creek of the Carew River in Wales.*

## WALES

*c.*1560 Sir Richard Clough builds Bachecraig, Denbigh, celebrated as the first classical country house in Wales.

*c.*1575 Sir John Perrot rebuilds Carew Castle in Dyfed.

*c.*1580 Sir John also rebuilds Laugharne Castle in South Wales. He was given the castle by Queen Elizabeth I in 1575.

1587–92 Sir Edward Herbert builds a splendid Long Gallery as part of major rebuilding at Powis Castle.

*Above: Killyleagh Castle is the oldest occupied castle in Ireland.*

## NORTHERN IRELAND

Dunluce Castle

North Channel

NORTHERN IRELAND

Springhill House

Antrim Castle

Tully Castle

Enniskillen Castle

Roughan Castle

Monea Castle

Castle Balfour

Killyleagh Castle

IRELAND

Irish Sea

1611 Capt Willam Cole rebuilds Enniskillen Castle in Co Fermanagh.

1616 Rev Malcolm Hamilton builds Monea Castle in Co Fermanagh.

1620 Randall MacDonnell, 1st Earl of Antrim, builds a manor house within Dunluce Castle, Co Antrim.

1680 Springhill House, a 'Plantation' house, is built by William Conyngham in Co Londonderry.

# THE MONARCHS

This list of monarchs names the kings and queens of Britain from the time of the ancient rulers of England and Scotland to the present day.

Much of the monarchy's authority and prestige derives from its ancient roots, from the centuries of historical continuity celebrated in genealogical and dynastic tables. Yet there are countless examples of force of arms and political manoeuvring intervening in dynastic or designated succession. The Wars of the Roses ended when Henry VII, the first monarch of the Tudor dynasty, won the English crown in battle against Richard III. Henry VII was the grandson of Owen Tudor, whose wife, Catherine of Valois, was the widow of Henry V. Although his claim to the throne rested in part on this, it was his victory at the Battle of Bosworth Field in 1485 that brought about an end to 30 years of dynastic warfare.

Throughout these and many other upheavals, the theory of dynastic succession with God's blessing was maintained. During the reign of Henry VII's son, Henry VIII, providing an heir and a stable succession became one of the key notes of the House of Tudor. His children, Edward VI, Mary I and Elizabeth I reigned during a time of religious turmoil as the European Reformation marked the rise of Protestantism.

The royal house of Stewart ruled in Scotland from 1371 onwards. By the time King James VI of Scotland became James I of England in 1603, the name was spelled Stuart. In England the early Stuart kings' authoritarianism led to clashes with Parliament and the execution of James's son, Charles I, in 1649. With the Restoration in 1660 and the reign of Charles II came the beginnings of a new relationship between the people and their king that led eventually to the establishment of a constitutional monarchy in the late 17th century.

## KINGS AND QUEENS OF SCOTLAND (TO 1603)

### THE HOUSE OF MACALPINE
Kenneth I mac Alpin 841–859
Donald I 859–863
Constantine I 863–877
Aed Whitefoot 877–878
Eochaid 878–889 (joint)
Giric 878–889
Donald II Dasachtach 889–900
Constantine II 900–943
Malcolm I 943–954
Indulf 954–962
Dubh 962–967
Culen 967–971
Kenneth II 971–995
Constantine III 995–997
Kenneth III 997–1005
Malcolm II 1005–1034

### THE HOUSE OF DUNKELD
Duncan I 1034–1040
Macbeth 1040–1057
Lulach 1057–1058
Malcolm III Canmore 1058–1093
Donald III 1093–1094
Duncan II 1094
Donald III 1094–1097 (joint)

*Above: James IV of Scotland presenting arms to his wife Queen Margaret, daughter of King Henry VII of England.*

Edmund 1094–1097 (joint)
Edgar 1097–1107
Alexander I 1107–1124
David I 1124–1153
Malcolm IV the Maiden 1153–1165
William I the Lion 1165–1214
Alexander II 1214–1249
Alexander III 1249–1286
Margaret, Maid of Norway 1286–1290

### THE HOUSE OF BALLIOL
John Balliol 1292–1296

### THE HOUSE OF BRUCE
Robert I the Bruce 1306–1329
David II 1329–1332, 1338–1371

### THE HOUSE OF BALLIOL
Edward Balliol 1332–1336

### THE HOUSE OF STEWART
Robert II 1371–1390
Robert III 1390–1406
James I 1406–1437
James II 1437–1460
James III 1460–1488
James IV 1488–1513
James V 1513–1542
Mary, Queen of Scots 1542–1567
James VI 1567–1603

*Below: King David II of Scotland (left) makes peace with King Edward III of England, in 1357.*

## KINGS AND QUEENS OF ENGLAND

**THE HOUSE OF WESSEX**
Egbert (802–839)
Aethelwulf (839–858)
Aethelbald (858–860)
Aethelbert (860–865/6)
Aethelred I (865/6–871)
Alfred the Great (871–899)
Edward the Elder (899–924/5)
Athelstan (924/5–939)
Edmund I (939–946)
Eadred (946–955)
Eadwig (955–959)
Edgar (959–975)
Edward the Martyr (975–978)
Aethelred II the Unready (978–1013, 1014–1016)
Edmund Ironside (1016)

*Above: King John goes riding. Hunting was the sport of kings from William I.*

**THE DANISH LINE**
Cnut (1016–1035)
Harald I Hardrada (1035–1040)
Harthacnut (1040–1042)

**THE HOUSE OF WESSEX, RESTORED**
Edward the Confessor (1042–1066)
Harold II (1066)

**THE NORMANS**
William I the Conqueror (1066–1087)
William II Rufus (1087–1100)
Henry I (1100–1135)
Stephen (1135–1154)

**THE PLANTAGENETS**
Henry II (1154–1189)
Richard I the Lionheart (1189–1199)
John (1199–1216)
Henry III (1216–1272)
Edward I (1272–1307)
Edward II (1307–1327)
Edward III (1327–1377)
Richard II (1377–1399)

**THE HOUSE OF LANCASTER**
Henry IV (1399–1413)
Henry V (1413–1422)
Henry VI (1422–1461, 1470–1471)

**THE HOUSE OF YORK**
Edward IV (1461–1470, 1471–1483)
Edward V (1483)
Richard III (1483–1485)

**THE HOUSE OF TUDOR**
Henry VII (1485–1509)
Henry VIII (1509–1547)
Edward VI (1547–1553)
Lady Jane Grey (1553)
Mary I (1553–1558)
Elizabeth I (1558–1603)

*Left: The heraldic badges of Kings Edward III, Richard II and Henry IV from Writhe's Garter Book.*

## KINGS AND QUEENS OF GREAT BRITAIN

**THE HOUSE OF STUART**
James I (1603-1625)
Charles I (1625-1649)
Charles II (1660-1685)
James II (1685-1688)
William III and Mary II (1689-1694)
William III (1689-1702)
Anne (1702-1714)

**THE HOUSE OF HANOVER**
George I (1714-1727)
George II (1727-1760)
George III (1760-1820)
George IV (1820-1830)
William IV (1830-1837)
Victoria (1837-1901)

**THE HOUSE OF SAXE-COBURG-GOTHA**
Edward VII (1901-1910)

**THE HOUSE OF WINDSOR**
George V (1910-1936)
Edward VIII (1936)
George VI (1936-1952)
Elizabeth II (1952-)

*Below: The Archbishop of Canterbury reverently places the crown on George V's head at the coronation in 1911.*

WAY IN

# CHAPTER ONE

# EARLY TUDOR PALACES AND COUNTRY HOUSES

### 1485–*c*.1550

At Hampton Court Palace in August 1546, Henry VIII made a bold statement of the glory of the youthful Tudor dynasty and his own regal largesse when he laid on feasts and entertainments for the French ambassador, a 200-strong body of French followers and 1,300 English courtiers. In the ten years *c*.1530-40, Henry had spent a massive £62,000 (around £18 million in today's money) on improving Hampton Court, already a glorious Renaissance-style palace built by Cardinal Thomas Wolsey in 1514-18.

At Hampton Court – and in a host of now ruined or demolished Tudor palaces – Henry's lavishly funded royal building expressed the magnificence of both Crown and state. Following his break with the Church of Rome and the establishment of the Church of England, the nation's greatest buildings were increasingly secular rather than sacred.

This new wave of secular building was funded in large part by the Dissolution of the Monasteries, when in the 1530s Henry suppressed England's great religious houses and seized their lands and wealth. The Crown's loyal servants and Henry's associates – such as Sir William Compton, builder of Compton Wynyates, and William Sandys, builder of The Vyne – were rewarded with grants of land and office that made them rich. In their service, English masons, woodworkers and glaziers who would once have worked for the Church exercised their skills in building the fine country houses of the early Tudor period.

*Left: The Gateway in the Tudor West Front at Hampton Court Palace was begun by Cardinal Wolsey and finished by Henry VIII.*

# COMPTON WYNYATES
## AND THE VYNE

 The delightful red-brick manor house of Compton Wynyates, in Warwickshire, was begun by Edmund Compton in 1481, just prior to the accession of the House of Tudor. Edmund's sturdy but good-looking country house was given some elegant additions, including a porch and some towers, by his son, the prominent Tudor courtier, Sir William Compton, between 1493 and 1528.

### EDMUND COMPTON'S MANOR

The house's name has an uncertain derivation: 'Compton' certainly means 'dwelling in the coombe (valley)'; but 'Wynyates' may refer either to the vineyards that once were planted in the area or to the nearby gap in the hills ('wind gate'?), where a windmill was built.

The Compton family had lived in the area since the early years of the 13th century and built an earlier manor house that Edmund Compton redeveloped. He kept little but the moat and its drawbridge from the earlier house when he built a new dwelling of four wings, enclosing a courtyard, with walls 4ft (1.2m) thick, and an impressive Big Hall with a linen-fold panelling screen and a gallery. Edmund used attractive raspberry-coloured bricks that give the

*Above: In its idyllic setting, and with the soft glow of its bricks, Compton Wynyates is one of England's most attractive houses.*

house an unforgettable glow against the greenery of the garden and the surrounding countryside. He dug a second, outer, moat – probably never filled with water – with its own drawbridge.

### SIR WILLIAM COMPTON

Edmund Compton died in 1491 and his son, William, became a ward of the Crown. From the age of 11, William served at court as a page to Prince Henry, the future King Henry VIII, and in later life remained a great friend of

that charismatic king. William fought, jousted and banqueted alongside his royal master, as well as romancing the ladies of the court. Henry knighted William at the Battle of Tournai, in 1512, and, as a sign of special favour, allowed him to add the royal lion of England to the Compton coat of arms.

At Compton Wynyates, *c*.1515, Sir William built a grand entrance porch and chapel, while adding a tower at each of the four corners of the house. The entrance porch was carved with the royal arms alongside the Latin inscription *Dom Rex Henricus Octav* ('My Master King Henry VIII'). He also installed the Big Hall's timber ceiling and great bay window, fitted with heraldic glass; both these came from the ruins of Fulbrooke Castle, near

*Left: Rich in tradition and history, Compton Wynyates has fine gardens and flowering plants climbing its red walls.*

Warwick, which he had been given by the King as a reward for his brave and loyal service.

### KING HENRY VIII'S ROOM

Among the rooms at Compton Wynyates, King Henry VIII's Room is of particular interest. Here, the monarch stayed on several occasions, and the stained-glass window features the royal arms and those of Aragon (birthplace of Queen Catherine). In later years, Queen Elizabeth I slept in the same room in 1572, while King James I stayed there in 1617. James made Sir William Compton 1st Earl of Northampton. Charles I, a close friend of Spencer Compton, 2nd Earl of Northampton, also stayed here. The ceiling (of 1625) contains the monograms of all the room's royal residents.

### LATER DEVELOPMENTS

During the Civil War, the Comptons remained staunch Royalists. The 2nd Earl fought at the battle of Edgehill in 1642 and was killed at the Battle of

---

### THE VYNE, HAMPSHIRE

The prominent Tudor courtier, William Sandys, built the manor house of The Vyne, in Hampshire, *c.*1500–20. It was built of attractive rose-coloured brick, with corner towers and tall windows across the main fronts, but had no moat or internal courtyard. Sandys became Lord Sandys in 1523 and was made Lord Chamberlain in Henry VIII's household in 1526. Henry visited The Vyne in 1510, 1531 and 1535, the third time with his new wife, Anne Boleyn. Lord Sandys died in 1540. Later owners of his house included Chaloner Chute (a Speaker of the House of Commons), who hired John Webb to build a classical portico, the earliest in an English country house, on The Vyne's north front (see also page 78).

*Below: The placing of the original windows was more haphazard than the symmetrical arrangement of the later sash windows.*

*Above: All who entered Sir William Compton's home walked beneath the motto "My Master King Henry VIII".*

Hopton Heath in 1643. In June 1644, Compton Wynyates was besieged and taken by the Parliamentarian army. In 1645, the Comptons tried but failed to retake the house and then fled into exile, where they remained until the Restoration. In line with their usual policy of slighting royalist fortifications, the Parliamentarians took the action of filling in the house's moat.

In later years, Compton Wynyates was uninhabited. The house decayed and came close to complete ruin. Indeed, in 1768 Lord Northampton ordered its demolition, but his agent fortunately did not carry out his instructions. In the later 19th century, Compton Wynyates was restored and from 1884 was once again inhabited, by the 5th Marquess of Northampton and his wife.

# HAMPTON COURT PALACE
## AND THE COURT OF HENRY VIII

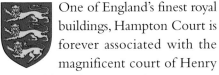

One of England's finest royal buildings, Hampton Court is forever associated with the magnificent court of Henry VIII, although major changes were made in the 17th century during the reign of William and Mary (see pages 82–3). The palace came into royal hands as a gift from the statesman, Cardinal Wolsey, to his royal master, Henry VIII.

### WOLSEY'S PALACE
In 1514, Wolsey, Lord Chancellor and Archbishop of York, obtained the lease of the building from the religious order of the Knights Hospitaliers of St John of Jerusalem. In five years of lavishly funded redevelopment, he transformed the Knights' relatively modest country retreat into a splendid and extensive palace. The eastern part of the kitchen range and the nearby Base Court, a guest courtyard surrounded by private accommodation for 40 or so visitors, remain essentially as they were in Wolsey's time.

*Below: The 19th-century artist Joseph Nash imagines Wolsey entertaining his lord and king at Hampton Court Palace.*

*Above: The turrets flanking the gatehouse in the Tudor West Front at Hampton Court hold roundels with the heads of Roman emperors.*

Recent archaeological research has shown that Wolsey's palace was laid out in a great geometric design that formed two eight-pointed stars, one beside the other. The magnificent design followed very closely the instructions in an Italian book of 1510, Paolo Cortese's *de Cardinalatu*, which described the dimensions and features of a perfect Cardinal's residence. Wolsey's flamboyant house was therefore England's first Italian Renaissance palace.

*Above: Wolsey laid out the first gardens at Hampton Court, then Henry VIII began a major redevelopment of them in 1529.*

In 1528, Wolsey was falling swiftly out of royal favour because he was unable to provide Henry VIII with a divorce from Catherine of Aragon. He attempted to halt this alarming slide by making a gift of his precious palace to Henry VIII. The ploy did not work: Henry happily accepted the gift of Hampton Court and almost at once launched his own major building projects there, but Wolsey's reputation was not restored.

Henry built extravagant royal suites, a beautiful chapel, an enormous Great Hall and 36,000sq ft (3,300sq m) of kitchens. He provided a vast lavatory complex that could be used by 28 people at one time, with water piped through 3 miles (5km) of lead piping. He laid out 1,100 acres (445ha) of hunting grounds, a large pleasure garden, tennis courts and a bowling alley.

### ELTHAM PALACE
Another of Henry VIII's favourite residences was Eltham Palace, once a manor house in the Kent countryside, now enveloped by south London. Given in 1295 by Anthony Bek, Bishop of Durham, to the future Edward II, Eltham became a much-frequented royal

## LOST PALACES OF THE TUDOR KINGS

Several other major Tudor palaces have been lost to posterity. Nonsuch Palace, near Ewell in Surrey, was so called because it was beyond compare – there was 'none such' anywhere else.

The Tudor palace at Greenwich was knocked down in the 17th century and replaced by the Queen's House and what is now the National Maritime Museum, designed by Inigo Jones and Sir Christopher Wren. The once-magnificent

*Below: A French chateau in Surrey. Henry VIII's Nonsuch Palace, near Ewell, was a magnificent sight in its Tudor prime.*

Richmond Palace, beside the Thames on the site of the former Sheen Palace in Surrey, collapsed into ruins.

Nothing remains of Baynard's Castle, which once stood near Upper Thames Street in the City of London. It was extended in the reign of Edward VI and frequented by Elizabeth I, but it burnt down in the Great Fire of London of 1666. Little also remains of Henry VIII's Bridewell Palace (once south of Fleet Street in London), or of his Whitehall Palace, also in central London, or of his Oatlands Palace near Weybridge in Surrey, where he loved to go hunting.

*Above: The cavernous Great Hall at Hampton Court, built by Henry VIII, has a magnificent hammer-beam roof.*

new west front. But the palace began to fall into decline in the early 17th century, then was occupied and ransacked by Parliamentary soldiers during the Civil War. In the 1930s, the Great Hall was restored and incorporated into a splendid new Art Deco house built by Stephen and Virginia Courtauld.

house in the 14th century. The French chronicler, Jean Froissart, described Eltham as 'a very magnificent palace', and the poet, Geoffrey Chaucer, as Clerk of the King's Works, was in charge of improvements carried out during Richard II's reign. In 1475–80, Edward IV built the magnificent Great Hall, with its splendid hammer-beam roof.

Henry VIII's reign saw the building of a new chapel and royal accommodation, and the laying out of gardens, an archery range and a bowling green. Elizabeth I gave the royal apartments a

*Right: The Great Hall of King Edward IV (c. 1470) stands to the left of the Courtaulds' 1930s house at Eltham Palace.*

# HEVER CASTLE
## THE HOME OF ANNE BOLEYN

The moated and fortified manor house of Hever Castle, near Edenbridge in Kent, was the childhood home of Anne Boleyn, mother of Elizabeth I. Henry VIII was a frequent visitor in the 1520s when he paid court to Anne.

### THE BOLEYNS

The first fortified building at Hever was built *c.*1270: the outer defensive wall and forbidding three-storey gatehouse date from this time. A century later, Sir John de Cobham added battlements and a moat complete with drawbridge. In 1459, Sir Geoffrey Bullen, a former Lord Mayor of London, bought the castle. After Sir Geoffrey's grandson, Sir Thomas, married Lady Elizabeth Howard, daughter of the Earl of Surrey, the family (now calling itself Boleyn) rose to prominence. Thomas served Henry VIII as an ambassador and as Treasurer of the King's Household; he was made a Knight of the Garter in

*Below: History breathes in the dining hall at Hever Castle, where Henry VIII paid court to the daughter of Sir Thomas Boleyn.*

*Above: In the early 16th century, Sir Thomas Boleyn, father of a future queen, built a Long Gallery at Hever Castle.*

1523 and Earl of Wiltshire in 1529. His two beautiful daughters, Mary and Anne, both served as ladies-in-waiting to Queen Catherine (of Aragon) and both caught the King's eye. Mary was Henry's mistress for a while, before she was eclipsed by Anne, who was beheaded three years after she became queen.

### CHANGES OF OWNERSHIP

Two years later, on Thomas's death, Hever Castle was taken over by the Crown. It was soon the possession of another royal, for Henry VIII gave it to Anne of Cleves on their divorce in

*Above: In her youth, Anne served at court abroad. Margaret, Archduchess of Austria, praised Anne as "bright and pleasant".*

1540, as he prepared to wed his fifth wife, Catherine Howard. After Anne's death in 1557, the castle reverted once more to the Crown until Mary Tudor made a gift of it to her courtier, Sir Edward Waldegrave. After many years of obscurity, the castle was bought in 1903 by the wealthy American financier William Waldorf Astor, who thoroughly renovated both house and estate.

### MOCK TUDOR

As part of his restoration of Hever, Astor refashioned the adjacent farm buildings into a Tudor-style village, using 16th-century timber from the dismantled Tudor stables. He laid out the gardens in Italian style, complete with grottoes and marble pavements, and excavated a 35-acre (13ha) lake. He meticulously restored the interior of the castle. In the dining room, he fitted the door with a lock that Henry VIII had carried with him to secure his sleeping chamber when he travelled, and, alongside it, an almost identical modern replica.

# LEEDS CASTLE
## AND ITS TRANSFORMATION BY HENRY VIII

Henry VIII took a great liking to Leeds Castle in Kent, and carried out lavish improvements, transforming it from castle to fortified palace. The King was often in Kent, where he was entertained at Penshurst Place and visited Anne Boleyn at Hever Castle. Leeds Castle had well-established royal links, and had been favoured by kings and queens since Edward I honeymooned there in 1299.

### HENRY'S ALTERATIONS

Henry entrusted the work at Leeds Castle to Sir Henry Guildford, who became Comptroller of the Royal Household. He added a storey to the Gloriette Tower on the northern island, installing large windows in the royal apartments there. He erected the Maidens' Tower as space for the maids of honour and refashioned the 75ft (23m) Banqueting Hall, adding a large bow window. The hall now contains a portrait of Henry VIII, and a splendid tapestry of the Magi, *c*.1490.

*Below: Henry VIII brought palatial luxury to Leeds Castle, in particular developing the Gloriette Tower and Banqueting Hall.*

*Above The Queens' Bedroom was first used by Henry V's wife, Catherine de Valois, who was the great grandmother of Henry VIII.*

As well as investing heavily in the comfort of Leeds Castle, Henry VIII took care to maintain its defences, for he was always aware of the threat of foreign invasion. Towards the end of his reign, Henry gave Leeds Castle to Sir Anthony St Leger as a reward for his service as Ireland's Lord Deputy. The

castle later belonged to John Culpeper, Chancellor of the Exchequer under King Charles I, and then to the Lords Fairfax. In the 20th century, the castle was restored by Lady Olive Baillie.

### TUDOR STYLE

By the 1530s and 1540s, memories of the Wars of the Roses were beginning to fade, and the new style in building celebrated the 'Tudor peace' by using increasing numbers of ever-larger windows. One feature particularly characteristic of Tudor houses is the oriel window, which projects out from an upper floor, supported from beneath by a bracket.

Tudor architectural style also moved away from the pointed Gothic arch to a flattened arch, subsequently known as the Tudor arch. Doors were smaller and more ornate, and houses were increasingly fitted with coal-burning fireplaces and chimneys. Within, many houses were fitted with wood panelling, often oak carved to resemble folded cloth, which was later known as 'linen-fold panelling'.

# THE TOWER OF LONDON
## A ROYAL PRISON AND PALACE

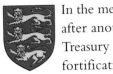 In the medieval era, one king after another dug deep into Treasury funds to strengthen fortifications at the Tower of London, while also developing the site as one of the capital city's royal palaces. Henry VIII enjoyed staying at the Tower, as well as despatching his enemies to the prison quarters there. He and his father, Henry VII, enlarged and improved royal accommodation in the Tower enclosure, but they were to be the last English monarchs to use it as a royal residence.

### MEDIEVAL FORTIFICATIONS

William Longchamp, Bishop of Ely, serving as regent while King Richard I was on Crusade, enlarged the Tower complex *c.*1190–1200, improving ditch defences to the north and east, building new sections of the wall and erecting the Bell Tower in the south-west. However, these new fortifications did not save Bishop William when the King's brother John besieged him there; through lack of provisions, the bishop was forced to surrender.

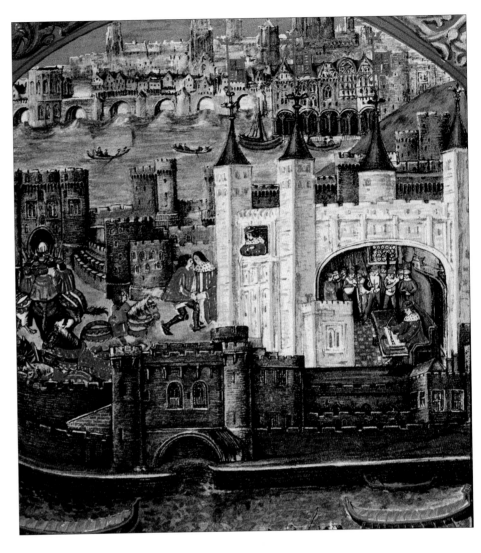

*Above: This 15th-century manuscript illumination is the earliest detailed image of the Tower. It depicts the imprisonment of Charles, Duke of Orléans.*

### MAJOR EVENTS AT THE TOWER

**1381** Richard II takes refuge in the Tower during the Peasants' Revolt.

**1399** Richard II renounces the crown in the White Tower and is succeeded by Henry IV.

**1465** and **1470** Edward IV holds court at the Tower.

**1471** Henry VI is imprisoned and probably murdered in the Wakefield Tower.

**1483** Richard III celebrates his coronation at the Tower; the 'Princes in the Tower', Edward V and his brother Richard, probably meet their end in the White Tower.

**1485** Henry VII holds his victory celebrations at the Tower after winning the crown at the Battle of Bosworth.

**1535–42** Henry VIII has many notable figures – including Sir Thomas More, Anne Boleyn, Thomas Cromwell and Catherine Howard – imprisoned in the Tower and then executed there.

**1554** Lady Jane Grey, queen for nine days, is executed on Tower Green on the orders of Mary I; Mary's half-sister, Princess Elizabeth (the future Elizabeth I), is imprisoned in the Tower.

**1601** Elizabeth I's former favourite, Robert Devereux, Earl of Essex, is the last person to be executed on Tower Green, having fallen out of favour with the Queen.

### DEFENSIVE TOWERS

In the early years of Henry III's reign, the Wakefield and Lanthorn towers were built on the riverfront, providing royal accommodation for king and queen respectively, while the Great Hall was extended and improved. In *c.*1238–41, Henry III built a new defensive wall along the east, north and west sides of the complex, with nine defensive towers (including the Devereux, Martin and Salt towers at the corners) and a moat on the outside filled from the Thames. Henry's improvements, which cost more

*Right: This aerial view of the Tower was made in 1597, late in Elizabeth I's reign, by William Haiward and J. Gascoyne.*

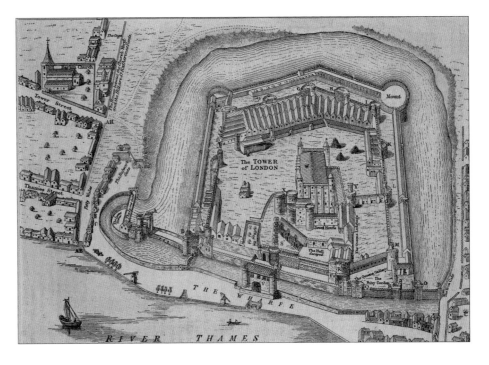

than £5,000, doubled the size of the Tower enclosure. He began regular use of the Tower as a prison and kept his extensive menagerie of animals there.

In 1275–85, Edward I further extended the enclosure, filling in his father's moat and building a second curtain wall to create concentric defences. Edward also built Beauchamp, Middle, Byward and St Thomas's towers, as well as a royal mint within the complex. Edward II did little further building work at the Tower, but he did move the royal accommodation from the Wakefield and St Thomas's towers to the Lanthorn Tower.

## TUDOR IMPROVEMENTS

Henry VIII carried out extensive improvements to royal lodgings at the Tower. His father, Henry VII, had enlarged the royal accommodation in the Lanthorn Tower, providing a Tudor Long Gallery, a private room and a Library, as well as a garden. Henry VIII liked to stay in the improved Lanthorn Tower. He also built additional royal lodgings near the White Tower, erected the half-timbered King's House, which can still be seen today in the inner bailey's south-west corner, and rebuilt the Chapel Royal of St Peter ad Vincula (St Peter in Chains).

Meanwhile, Thomas Cromwell improved the defences of the fortified complex, and in the reign of Henry VIII the Tower saw many celebrated prisoners go to their deaths. In the space of just seven years, Sir Thomas More, Cardinal John Fisher, Anne Boleyn, Thomas Cromwell and Catherine Howard were all imprisoned in the Tower before their execution.

*Above: Traitors' Gate – the riverbank water-gate at the foot of St Thomas's Tower – was built by Edward I in 1275–9.*

*Left: This view of the Tower from the river shows the Traitors' Gate in the centre foreground. All prisoners disembarked here and entered the Tower through this gate.*

# SULGRAVE MANOR
## AND GEORGE WASHINGTON'S FAMILY

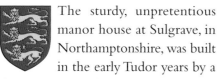

The sturdy, unpretentious manor house at Sulgrave, in Northamptonshire, was built in the early Tudor years by a direct ancestor of George Washington, the first President of the United States of America. Lawrence Washington, younger son of a prominent Lancashire family, was born *c*.1500. He became a wool merchant and bought the Priory of St Andrew, Northampton, from the Crown in 1539, following Henry VIII's Dissolution of the Monasteries.

*Below: The compact south front of Sulgrave Manor, built of local limestone by Lawrence Washington, faces a pleasant garden.*

**THE ORIGINAL BUILDING**

After his first wife, Elizabeth, died childless, Lawrence married Amy, daughter of landowner Robert Pargiter, and settled at Sulgrave, where he established Sulgrave Manor, which is a fine example of a smaller Tudor country house.

The house was built of local limestone, with a wide south frontage, a kitchen and buttery, a Great Hall, and above it a Great Chamber and two smaller private chambers. All these parts survive and can be seen today. Finds of what appear to have been Tudor-era foundation stones as much as 50ft (15m) west of the current house suggest that the original dwelling was considerably

*Above: George Washington, first President of the United States, traced his family roots to a Northamptonshire manor house.*

larger than the surviving house. The Great Hall has a stone floor, and its Tudor fireplace contains a salt cupboard carved with the initials of Lawrence Washington.

**'ER' AND STARS AND STRIPES**

Lawrence added an entrance porch to the house's south front after 1558. Over the doorway he set in plaster the royal arms of England and the letters 'ER', to indicate 'Elizabeth Regina' in honour of Henry VIII's daughter Elizabeth I, who had ascended to the throne. The doorway spandrels were decorated with the Washington family arms: two stripes and three stars. Some people have suggested that this design was one of the inspirations for the 'stars and stripes' of the American flag.

Lawrence's eldest son, Robert Washington, who was born in 1544, subsequently inherited Sulgrave Manor, along with 1,250 acres (506ha) of farmland. Robert was George Washington's great-great-great-great-grandfather.

## HELLEN'S, MUCH MARCLE

The charming country house of Hellen's in the Herefordshire village of Much Marcle near Ledbury was once known as Hellion's Home or Hellinham Castle. It was owned by the lords Audley, earls of Gloucester in the 14th century; a certain Walter Helyon leased the estate and gave his name to the house.

Hellen's lower and older wing contains a venerable Great Hall, refurbished after an 18th-century fire, with a chimney hood decorated with the emblems of the 'Black Prince', son of Edward III. According to tradition, this was fitted in the 14th century by James Audley, companion of the 'Black Prince'. The larger wing is Tudor and contains a splendid oak chimney-piece.

In the 16th century, the then occupier, a Roman Catholic named Richard Walwyn, decorated an upstairs room in this wing with gold and red brocade in honour of Mary Tudor, later Queen Mary I, who was staying nearby in Ludlow Castle. The fireplace is decorated with Mary's initials and coat of arms.

*Below: The Great Bedchamber is part of the original manor house rather than the 18th-century extension. This picture is c.1910.*

*Right: These stained-glass panels feature the Washington and Kitson arms and the Washington and Butler Arms, 1588.*

### LATER ALTERATIONS

A north wing, set at right angles to Lawrence Washington's manor, was added c.1700 by the then owner, John Hodges. It contains the Great Kitchen and the Oak Parlour, on the ground floor, beneath two sleeping chambers, now known as the White Bedroom and the Chintz Bedroom. Another extension, the west wing, was built in 1929 when the house was being restored.

### WASHINGTON'S DESCENDANTS

Lawrence Washington's grandson, another Lawrence, became a rector at Purleigh in Essex. But during the English Civil War, the staunchly royalist Reverend Washington was evicted by Parliament from his living, and died in poverty. His son, John, sailed to the English colony of Virginia in 1656 and married Anne Pope from the Cliffs, a settlement in northern Virginia. They held an estate of 700 acres (385ha) at Mattox Creek Farm. Their eldest son, Lawrence, became a member of Virginia's House of Burgesses and had three children by Mildred Warner. The second, Augustine, was the father of George Washington, the first US President, born on 22 February 1732.

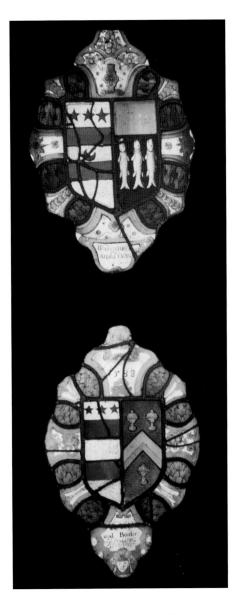

*Below: Honouring the Queen. The royal arms of England and the initials 'ER' decorate the south porch, added c.1560.*

# EDINBURGH CASTLE
## AND HOLYROODHOUSE

Edinburgh Castle was a well-established stronghold and royal dwelling by the latter years of the 14th century, when the future Robert II built David's Tower, containing royal apartments. In the mid-1430s, James I built a new Great Chamber, probably alongside the royal accommodation in the Tower. His successor, James II, brought the great siege gun of Mons Meg to the castle, which assumed an increasingly important role as a royal artillery.

### GREAT CHAMBER, GREAT HALL
James IV extended the royal accommodation into the southern part of the rocky summit on which the castle stands, reconstructed James I's Great Chamber and built a Great Hall. These two buildings stand along the east and south sides of a courtyard (now Crown Square), with the 14th-century St Mary's Church along the north side (now the Scottish National War Memorial) and artillery buildings to the west. The extended

*Below: James V built a Great Tower at the north-west corner of Holyroodhouse in 1528–32 and a new west front in 1535–6.*

Great Chamber had windows facing east, and must have provided fine views of the burgh below and the countryside beyond. The Great Hall was quite small, at 82 x 32ft (25 x 10m), because its size was limited by its location. It has large mullioned windows on the south side and a hammer-beam roof.

### HOLYROODHOUSE
Holyrood Palace was originally part of a monastery. David I founded the Augustinian Priory of the Holy Rude in 1128, and after Edinburgh was made the capital of Scotland in the 15th century, the abbey guest house (Holyroodhouse) was increasingly used

*Left: Edinburgh Castle, on its rocky summit, proved too small for a sufficiently grand royal base, so Scotland's kings instead developed Holyrood Abbey into a palace.*

by the royal family, eventually eclipsing the castle as the city's foremost royal residence (see page 74). Set among gardens and orchards, it provided more space and comfort than the cramped royal palace of Edinburgh Castle, perched on its rocky summit above the burgh.

James II was born in Holyroodhouse in October 1430, held his coronation and marriage in the abbey church and was buried there in 1460. James IV built a new palace at Holyrood in 1501–4, but little or nothing survives of this palace, which was extensively rebuilt by James V. In 1528–32, he built a great rectangular tower with round corner turrets as a royal lodging. This impressive building is still standing today in the palace front. Then, in 1535–6, he rebuilt the west wing of James IV's palace, and adapted the north and south wings.

*Below: The royal arms of James V of Scots sit proudly on the wall at Holyroodhouse. James was buried in the abbey in 1543.*

# FALKLAND PALACE
## AND STIRLING CASTLE

Falkland Palace began as a castle built by the Macduffs, earls of Fife, probably in the 13th century. James II extended the castle and frequently visited it to hunt deer and wild boar. After 1458, when he granted a charter, it was known as Falkland Palace. James IV built a new palace complex, to the south of the royal castle, in 1501–13; then James V remodelled and rebuilt it, using French and Italian craftsmen, in 1537–41, to create Scotland's first palace in the continental Renaissance style.

James IV's palace was laid out around a courtyard, with a Great Hall on the north side, royal apartments on the east side, and a chapel and vestry to the south; entry was from the west, providing access to the adjacent burgh. James V remodelled the eastern block, building a new front that led on to the courtyard, entirely reconstructing the southern (chapel) section and adding an impressive gatehouse at its west end, designed to function as a new entrance. He also built, in 1539, a real tennis court, to the north of the palace. This can still be seen today and is Scotland's oldest court. James V's daughter, Mary, Queen of Scots, was a frequent visitor to Falkland Palace after her return to Scotland from French exile in 1561.

*Below: At Stirling, James V's craftsmen brought the elegance of Italian-French Renaissance architecture to Scotland.*

### STIRLING CASTLE
At Stirling, James V built a magnificent Renaissance-style palace as part of the royal castle. The original castle was 11th-century and, as at Falkland, was extensively rebuilt by James IV, who built a vast Great Hall *c.*1498–1503, which measured 128 x 36ft (39 x 11m) and 54ft (16.5m) high, with no fewer than five fireplaces.

In 1538–42, his son, James V, built a lavish three-storey palace within the castle complex, containing apartments for himself and his queen, Mary of Guise. This included an extraordinary Royal Presence Chamber with a ceiling that originally had 100 carved oak heads, some of which survive. The building's principal façade contains tall, elegant windows and niches holding sculptured figures.

*Above: Elements of the design at Falkland derive from that of the chateau at Joinville, built by the Duke of Guise in c.1530–40.*

### RENAISSANCE STYLE
The courtyard façades of the eastern (royal accommodation) and southern (chapel) ranges at Falkland Palace feature bays with medallion heads, dormer windows and statuary. Together, these make an elegant exposition of the latest French-Italian Renaissance style that would have appealed to James V's French wives – first Madeleine of Valois and then Mary of Guise. Scholars compare the bay design to those of the chateaux of Fontainebleu and Villers-Cotterêts, owned by Madeleine's father, the French king, Francis I.

# DEAL CASTLE
## COASTAL DEFENCES

 Henry VIII built the low-lying artillery fort of Deal Castle, in Kent, as one of a string of coastal fortifications built around England's south coast in the later 1530s and early 1540s. Following his break with the Church of Rome, he feared invasion by the armies of a Franco-Spanish Catholic alliance brokered by the Pope.

### SOUTH-COAST FORTS

Henry built three forts at Sandown, Deal and Walmer to cover anchorage off the Downs coast. They were built in 18 months using press-ganged labour and stone from local religious houses suppressed by the Dissolution of the Monasteries, including the former Carmelite priory at Sandwich. Earth bulwarks linked the three forts into a single defensive system. Today, little remains of the Sandown fort, and the

*Below: Tudor rose or double clover? The coastal fort at Deal in Kent has an impressive outline when viewed from the air.*

*Above: In the late 1530s, when he built these forts, Henry VIII was in his late 40s, less than a decade from his death (1547).*

defences at Walmer were later transformed into a splendid coastal residence, the official dwelling of the Lord Warden of the Cinque Ports, and the place where the Duke of Wellington, holder of this position, died in 1852. But the fort of Deal stands almost exactly as

Henry VIII built it – with the exception of some battlements added in the mid-18th century.

### THE TUDOR ROSE

Deal Castle is best viewed from the air. It was designed with a central circular tower and two tiers of semicircular bastions, giving the whole the shape of a double clover-leaf or Tudor rose. The circular walls had the advantage of deflecting cannon shot better than flat ones with vulnerable corners. The fort stood within a wide and deep moat, crossed by a drawbridge. Its entrance was formidable, with a portcullis, five murder-holes giving on to the entrance passageway from above, and an extremely thick oak door studded with iron.

The castle was a vast gun fortification with more than 200 cannon and gun ports, yet it was designed to be garrisoned by just 24 men plus a captain. They were equipped to withstand a siege: the basement contained a well and storage areas for food and drink, while the ground floor housed a bakery

*Above: At Pendennis Castle in Cornwall, the gun tower rises above the two-storey block containing the castellan's rooms.*

and kitchen. Also on the ground floor were living quarters for the garrison, with more spacious accommodation on the first floor for the captain and also his senior subordinates.

Deal Castle fulfilled its intended primary role as a deterrent and was not attacked in the 1530s. In fact, the only military action it has seen in its entire history was in the English Civil War, when, originally garrisoned by Parliamentarians, it surrendered to Royalists, and then was besieged and recaptured with a loss of 80 Royalist lives in August 1648.

### CORNISH STRONGHOLDS

Henry's coastal forts also included two handsome examples on Falmouth Bay in Cornwall: Pendennis Castle and St Mawes Castle, guarding the entrance to the River Fal estuary. Pendennis Castle was built in 1540–45: it was a keep within a curtain wall on Pendennis Head, with a smaller fortification, Little Dennis, on the rocks at the foot of the promontory. The keep combined a three-storey circular gun tower with a two-storey

rectangular block that contained the accommodation for the castle governor. These buildings were enclosed by a low but stoutly defended curtain wall, and the entrance to the castle was via a drawbridge across a dry moat and guarded by a portcullis.

The headland was enclosed by an outer curtain wall, creating a 4-acre (1.6ha) enclosure, in 1598. This followed Spanish sea raids on Cornwall in 1595 and was carried out amid fears that plans were afoot for a second Armada on the tenth anniversary of the first.

Across the bay, St Mawes Castle consisted of a circular gun tower with

three semicircular bastions around it so that, from above, the structure looked like a clover-leaf. Cannon were positioned on the roof of the tower and on the bastions, and also within the buildings to be fired through gun ports.

### THE SIEGE OF PENDENNIS

Pendennis Castle was the last Royalist fort in England to surrender during the Civil War. Sir Thomas Fairfax and the Parliamentarian New Model Army arrived in Cornwall in early March 1646 and took St Mawes Castle without a fight on 12 March. But when he came to Pendennis Castle and demanded the surrender of the garrison, the 70-year-old castle commander, Colonel John Arundell, defiantly declared: 'The Castle was entrusted to my government by His Majesty…. my age of 70 calls me hence shortly…. I shall desire no other testimony to follow my departure than my…loyalty to His Majesty…. I resolve that I will here bury myself before I deliver up this Castle to those who fight against His Majesty.' The siege began, and remarkably the castle, although blockaded by sea and land, survived for nearly five months before surrendering on 17 August. Two days later, Royalist Raglan Castle in Wales also surrendered.

*Below: St Mawes Castle was vulnerable to a land attack, but was in an ideal position for defending against invasion by sea.*

# SYON HOUSE
## AND SUDELEY CASTLE

The splendid Syon House, now surrounded by London's westward sprawl at Brentford in Middlesex, was built during the reign of Edward VI by his uncle Edward, Duke of Somerset, Lord Protector. Somerset built a three-storey building with battlements and angle turrets around a central courtyard. His house stood on the foundations of the abbey church that had belonged to the convent on the site.

The Lord Protector also established one of England's first botanical gardens at Syon House, in the care of his personal physician, Dr William Turner.

*Below: The 'Wizard' Earl built this superb 136ft (41m) Long Gallery at Syon House in the late 1500s. The sumptuous décor was designed by Robert Adam in the 1760s.*

While working on the garden at Syon House, Dr Turner wrote *The Names of Herbes*, published in 1548. Dr Turner is believed to have planted the mulberry trees, introduced to England from Persia (modern Iran) only half a century earlier, that still thrive at Syon House.

### A COLOURFUL HISTORY
The land on which Syon House was built had originally belonged to a Bridgettine convent, founded at Twickenham by Henry V in 1415. In the 1530s, the nuns' father confessor, Richard Reynolds, refused to accept Henry VIII's new status as Supreme Head of the Church of England and was brutally executed, his body later placed on the gateway to the abbey. Henry dissolved the Syon convent – named in honour of Mount Zion – and took possession

of the building and lands in 1539. He incarcerated his fifth queen, Catherine Howard, at Syon House prior to her execution in 1542. After his death in 1547, Henry's coffin rested overnight at Syon *en route* from Westminster to Windsor. The next morning, the coffin was found to have burst open, and dogs were gnawing the royal corpse. Some people regarded this as divine retribution for Henry's desecration of the abbey.

Somerset was ousted as Lord Protector in 1549 and executed on trumped-up treason charges in 1552. His successor, John Dudley, Duke of Northumberland, took possession of Syon House. At Syon, Northumberland's daughter-in-law, Lady Jane Grey, agreed to the plan to make her queen on the death of Edward VI. When this scheme

## SUDELEY CASTLE, GLOUCESTERSHIRE

The 15th-century Sudeley Castle in Gloucestershire was rebuilt in the late 1540s by Lord Thomas Seymour. Thomas was the brother of the Duke of Somerset, Lord Protector to Edward VI;

*Below: Henry VIII, Elizabeth I and Charles I all paid visits to Sudeley. Charles's nephew Prince Rupert had his headquarters there in the Civil War.*

their sister, Jane, had been Henry VIII's third wife, who had died giving birth to Edward in 1537, making the brothers the young king's uncles. In addition, Thomas married Henry VIII's sixth wife and widow, Catherine Parr, following the King's death.

Thomas and Catherine moved into Sudeley Castle, where they built a new set of rooms for Catherine's use. She gave birth at Sudeley to Lord Thomas's

*Above: Sudeley Castle's 14 acres (6ha) of gardens have been lovingly redeveloped.*

daughter, Mary, on 30 August 1548, but died of puerperal fever a week later and was buried in St Mary's Church near the castle.

After Lord Thomas Seymour's execution for treason in 1549, Sudeley Castle eventually passed into the hands of John Brydges, Lord Chandos, who entertained Elizabeth I at the castle three times.

failed, and Edward was succeeded by his sister, Queen Mary I, Northumberland, his son, Lord Guildford Dudley, and Lady Jane herself were all executed.

The Bridgettine nuns briefly came back from exile to live at Syon House under Mary I's rule, but in 1558 were banished once more. Then, in 1594, Syon House came into the possession of Henry Percy, 9th Earl of Northumberland, whose descendants still own the house today.

### THE 'WIZARD' EARL

Henry redecorated Syon House internally, built new stables and erected a fine Tudor Long Gallery. Nicknamed 'the Wizard' because of his experiments with alchemy, he was a great scholar, friend of Sir Walter Raleigh and acquaintance of Shakespeare, Ben Jonson and Sir Edmund Spenser. However, on 4 November 1605, he entertained at Syon House a Roman

Catholic cousin, Thomas Percy, who was implicated in the following day's 'Gunpowder Plot' to blow up the Houses of Parliament. Considered guilty by association, Northumberland was thrown into the Tower of London by James I, where he remained for 15 years.

His son Algernon, 10th Earl of Northumberland, commissioned Inigo Jones to design and build an arcade on Syon House's east side. The 10th Earl served as governor of Charles I's son James, Duke of York (the future James II); in 1646, the King's children stayed at Syon House to escape the London plague. The 10th Earl was a great patron of the arts, notably of the artists Sir Anthony van Dyck and Sir Peter Lely.

### A NEW LOOK

A little over a century later, in the 1760s, the 1st Duke of Northumberland commissioned Robert Adam to redesign the interior of Syon House. He hired

'Capability' Brown to refashion the park. The Duke had inherited the estate through his marriage to the Percy heiress Elizabeth Seymour in 1750. He felt that Syon House, which he considered 'ruinous and inconvenient', needed thoroughly remodelling.

*Below: Somerset built Syon House as a castle dwelling, with battlements and turrets. It sits in 40 acres (16ha) of gardens.*

# CHAPTER TWO

# 'PRODIGY HOUSES': THE AGE OF GLORIANA

### c.1550–1600

In 1555, leading Elizabethan statesman Sir William Cecil began building a country mansion sufficiently grand to receive and entertain his queen, Elizabeth I. He spared no effort and no expense in creating the magnificent Burghley House in Lincolnshire. At around the same time, his fellow courtier and friend Sir Christopher Hatton was building a similarly extravagant house at Holdenby in Northamptonshire.

Cecil and Hatton were not unusual. Several Elizabethan noblemen sank their wealth into the creation of 'prodigy houses' – country palaces fit for the Queen. Sir William More rebuilt his manor house of Loseley House in Surrey, reputedly on the instructions of Elizabeth herself; the Queen's great favourite, Robert Dudley, Earl of Leicester, lavished funds on Kenilworth Castle in Warwickshire in order to welcome his royal patron there; Sir John Thynne built the magnificent Longleat House in Wiltshire; and Sir Francis Willoughby sank his fortune into the extravagantly ornamented Wollaton Hall in Nottinghamshire. However, not all these houses achieved their objective. Sir William Cecil entertained Elizabeth and her court on 12 occasions at Burghley and his other houses. Elizabeth was entertained at Kenilworth Castle on several occasions, visited Longleat House even before it was finished and stayed at Loseley House at least twice. Yet, despite being a royal favourite, Sir Christopher Hatton – for all his devoted expenditure on Holdenby – was never honoured by a visit from the 'Virgin Queen'.

*Left: A house, a prodigy – but not a home. Sir William Cecil was at court so much that he seldom lived at Burghley House.*

# BURGHLEY HOUSE
## 'E' FOR ELIZABETH

Sir William Cecil built his extravagant 'prodigy house' on the Burghley estate, which his father, Richard Cecil, had purchased after it had been seized from Peterborough Abbey on the Dissolution of the Monasteries under Henry VIII. Construction took 32 years, from 1555 to 1587.

During this period, Cecil proved an indispensable adviser to Elizabeth I, establishing himself as the leading politician of his day. Born in 1520, he had begun his career as secretary to the Protector, Edward Seymour, Duke of Somerset, during Edward VI's reign; on Elizabeth's accession in 1558, he was appointed Secretary of State, then made 1st Baron Burghley in 1571 and Lord High Treasurer in 1572.

### A GIANT 'E'

Cecil was often absent from Burghley House, for his court and diplomatic responsibilities kept him very busy, but the building work was carried out largely according to his designs – with some assistance from a certain Henryk,

### PATRONS AND BUILDERS

The great houses of the Elizabethan era did not have architects in the sense in which we use the word. The people responsible for the shape the houses took were the master masons, the surveyors and their patrons, who commissioned the building. The patrons – renowned figures such as Sir William Cecil, Sir Thomas Thynne of Longleat House and Bess of Hardwick, who built Hardwick Hall in Derbyshire – were intimately involved in the design and construction process. The houses were often the three-dimensional stone embodiment of a 'device' or conceit: Burghley House was a giant 'E' to honour Elizabeth, while Hardwick Hall was a Greek cross doubled with a square placed upon it. Such a 'device' would have been the idea of the patron, in a sense their signature, an expression of their character, a

*Right: Statesman amd patron. Men such as William Cecil saw a great house as a lasting expression of their character and wit.*

statement of their intellectual and artistic prowess. The surveyors and master masons were charged with bringing these ideas into three solid dimensions. Among the surveyors, the greatest was Robert Smythson, who oversaw the building of many of the finest 'prodigy houses', including Longleat House, Hardwick Hall and Wollaton Hall.

an Antwerp mason. In *c.*1555–65, Cecil raised the east side of the house, then proceeded in 1577–87 to lay out the remainder of the house in the shape of a long courtyard, with a Great Hall at one end and a grand gatehouse at the other. The unusually high Great Hall was built with a splendid double-hammer-beam roof and notably elongated windows. Overall, the house took the form of a giant letter 'E' in honour of Elizabeth, although this touch can no longer be appreciated because the north-west wing was demolished in the mid–18th century.

*Left: Burghley's size and roofline inspired Daniel Defoe's 1722 remark that it was 'more like a town than a house'.*

Few other alterations have been made to the exterior of Burghley House since the completion of Cecil's work. It has splendid façades of hard 'Barnack rag', a limestone quarried nearby in Northamptonshire, with great expanses of glass in its transomed and mullioned windows.

## COMPLEX ROOFSCAPE

Burghley has a distinctive silhouette because its skyline is crowded with chimneys, cupolas and obelisks. Its lead roofing covers ¾ acre (over 3,000sq m). When English novelist, Daniel Defoe, visited Burghley House in 1722, he was particularly struck by the roof, which made Burghley look 'more like a town than a house…the towers and pinnacles, so high and placed at such a great distance from one another, look like so many distant parish churches in a town, and a large spire covered with lead, over the clock in the centre, looks like the Cathedral, or chief Church of that town'.

## WEALTH OF ART

More than a century after its construction, Burghley's interior was transformed when Sir William Cecil's descendant, the 5th Earl of Exeter, embarked on a redecoration programme of the

public and most important private rooms in the Baroque style. Exquisite plaster ceilings, probably designed by Edward Martin, and delicate carved wood panelling by Thomas Young and Grinling Gibbons were installed. A series of ceiling and wall paintings by the Italian artist Antonio Verrio adorn the suite now known as the George Rooms. His most spectacular work is in the Heaven Room.

*Above: The George Rooms (so called because they were decorated for a visit by the Prince Regent) contain paintings by the great Italian baroque artist Antonio Verrio.*

The 5th and 9th Earls of Exeter, both great travellers and art collectors, amassed a remarkable collection of paintings now displayed in Burghley House. These include works by Pieter Brueghel, Rembrandt and Thomas Gainsborough, a portrait of Henry VIII by Joos van Cleve, portraits of the 5th Earl and of Antonio Verrio by Sir Godfrey Kneller, and a chapel altarpiece by Veronese.

## GATES AND GROUNDS

In the late 17th century, Frenchman Jean Tijou added splendid wrought-iron gates to the principal gatehouse. In the mid-18th century, the 9th Earl of Exeter commissioned Lancelot 'Capability' Brown, both as an architect and to landscape the 300-acre (120ha) park. At this time, the house's north-west wing was demolished to allow better views of Brown's parkland from the south front.

*Left: The vast kitchen at Burghley House dates back to Tudor times. It also contains 260 Georgian–Victorian copper utensils.*

# KENILWORTH CASTLE
## ELIZABETH AND LEICESTER

In 1563, Elizabeth I granted Kenilworth Castle, a 12th-century Norman stronghold in Warwickshire, to her great favourite, Robert Dudley, Earl of Leicester. He built a gatehouse and elegant residential quarters to make the historic fortifications sufficiently grand for the Queen. She visited him at Kenilworth Castle in 1566, 1568, 1572 and 1575.

### NORMAN ORIGINS

The original castle was built *c*.1122 by Geoffrey de Clinton, King Henry I's Chamberlain, on land granted to him by the King. Geoffrey built a simple motte-and-bailey castle, with a wooden tower enclosed by an earthwork bank. His works were remade in stone, probably by his son, Geoffrey de Clinton II, in the form of a two-storey stone keep with walls up to 20ft (6m) thick covering the original mound.

*Above: This aerial view of the ruins of Kenilworth Castle shows the remains of the ornamental gardens laid out by Leicester.*

*Below: A reconstruction of the estate in the time of Elizabeth I. Leicester's Kenilworth was more country house than castle.*

### WATER DEFENCES

The castle passed into royal hands, and was greatly extended in 1210–15 by King John, who built an outer wall with defensive towers and a fortified dam that blocked several local streams to create a wide lake around the castle that covered 100 acres (40ha). The water defences played a key role in 1266, during the civil war between King Henry III and his son, Prince Edward, and rebel lords led by Simon de Montfort. The castle had been given to de Montfort by Henry, and when civil war broke out, de Montfort's supporters were besieged by a royalist force. The defenders held out for nine months, finally surrendering with honour. Castle-builders were impressed by the effectiveness of the lake in preventing attackers tunnelling into the castle or undermining its walls.

### ONE HUNDRED KNIGHTS

In 1279, Kenilworth Castle was the scene of a famous jousting tournament held by Roger de Mortimer. In celebration of Arthurian chivalry, Roger established a 'Round Table' at the castle, and a company of 100 knights competed before an audience of 100 ladies on the lake dam.

## SHAKESPEARE AT KENILWORTH

According to popular tradition, an 11-year-old William Shakespeare travelled from Stratford-upon-Avon to nearby Kenilworth Castle to witness the extravagant theatrical pageantry laid on by the Earl of Leicester for Queen Elizabeth in July 1575.

As part of the extravaganza, Elizabeth watched, and apparently greatly enjoyed, a performance of a play, *The Slaughter of the Danes at Hock Tide*, by an acting troupe named 'The Men of Coventry';

*Above: Leicester and Elizabeth – an earl courts a queen in a summer garden. The Arcadian romance that inspired Shakespeare touches the English soul.*

there were 'Arcadian' pageants featuring figures from classical mythology and English folklore. Some writers suggest that the magic of Shakespeare's play *A Midsummer Night's Dream* derives in part from his treasured memories of the Queen's visit to Kenilworth Castle.

---

The earls of Lancaster came into possession of the castle, and in 1389–94 Edward III's son John of Gaunt, 1st

*Below: John of Gaunt's Hall (left) and Leicester's Buildings (right) sandwich the Saintlowe Tower (part of the Great Hall).*

Duke of Lancaster, built a magnificent Great Hall and luxurious accommodation in the castle's inner ward. His grandson, Henry V, built a banqueting house at the end of the lake, or Great Mere. Henry VIII later rebuilt this house within the castle precincts.

### LEICESTER'S ALTERATIONS

After receiving the castle from Queen Elizabeth I, the Earl of Leicester created a grand entrance via a gatehouse to the north, added numerous windows to the keep, in the process of updating it to make it suitable for entertaining rather than siege defence, and built a residential suite (later known as Leicester's Buildings) to the south of the inner curtain wall. He also laid out a formal Elizabethan garden within the outer bailey.

In 1575, as part of her 'summer progress' around her kingdom, Elizabeth stayed at Kenilworth for 18 days, being entertained at Leicester's expense with pageants, jousting, dancing, theatrical shows, hunting and feasting. Leicester gave Elizabeth an entire wing and even had a garden laid out beneath her bedroom window when she complained of not being able to see the castle gardens from her private chambers. The visit reputedly cost Leicester £1,000 per day.

### THE LOSS OF THE LAKE

During the Civil War, Parliamentary forces took the castle, and afterwards the north curtain wall and the keep's north wall were destroyed and the water defences drained. In later years, the castle crumbled into a romantic ruin, with only Leicester's gatehouse remaining habitable. The other major buildings, such as the keep and John of Gaunt's Great Hall, stood as evocative reminders of Kenilworth's importance in the Middle Ages and the Elizabethan age.

# CRATHES CASTLE
## AND THE SCOTTISH TOWER HOUSE

 Built by the Burnett family in 1553–94, Crathes Castle in Aberdeenshire is a commanding example of the 16th-century Scottish tower house. In England, the long years of the 'Tudor peace' allowed wealthy merchants and landowners to concentrate on comfort and beauty rather than fortification, to build unfortified country houses rather than castles. But in Scotland, where times remained more turbulent, landowners built tower houses, which combined defensive capabilities with domestic comfort.

Crathes was begun by Alexander Burnett, descendant of the powerful, originally Anglo-Saxon, Burnard family, who were rewarded for service to King Robert I the Bruce with the barony of Leys and the position of Royal Forester in the Forest of Drum. Family legend has

*Below: Generations of Burnetts poured their energies into building Crathes Castle. The family lived there until 1966.*

it that the Horn of Leys, an ivory hunting horn encrusted with jewels and now displayed in the High Hall of Crathes Castle, was given to a Burnett ancestor, also called Alexander, by the Bruce himself and came with the Forester's office. Crathes Castle was completed by yet another Alexander, great-grandson of the original builder.

### GRANITE TOWER

Crathes Castle is a great L-shaped granite tower, its rooms piled one on top of another. The lower parts of the granite walls are plain, and rise, tapering inwards slightly, to finish in a 'fairytale' explosion of gables, corbels and turrets at roof level.

The design of the tower house was dictated partly by defensive needs and partly by the shortage of wood in Scotland. Large roofs required a great deal of timber, so the tower house enclosed a large amount of living space beneath a small roof. At Crathes, the roof covers 1,800sq ft (548sq m); stone

vaulting rather than timber supports the whole of the first floor and most of the second. The High Hall, now floored with modern timber, originally had stone flags. Tower houses typically had a 'barmkin', or defensive wall, enclosing land at their base.

The tower at Crathes originally rose above a side wing erected to provide extra living space. This block was rebuilt as the Queen Anne Wing in the early 18th century by Thomas Burnett, who, as the father of 21 children, was in need of plentiful family accommodation. Thomas also removed the barmkin, planting Irish yew hedges and an avenue of lime trees in its place. These plantings formed the basis of a beautiful garden developed by Sir James and Lady Burnett in the early 20th century. Unfortunately, Thomas's other legacy, the Queen Anne Wing, burned down in 1966. It was replaced by a modern two-storey range.

### PAINTED CEILINGS

Crathes Castle is particularly notable for its original painted ceilings, seen to great advantage in the Chamber of the Muses, the Green Lady's Room and the Chamber of the Nine Worthies. The latter room, completed in 1602, features images of classical figures Julius Caesar, Alexander the Great and the ancient Greek hero, Hector; Old Testament figures Joshua, King David and Judas Maccabeus; and such legendary and historical figures as King Arthur, Charlemagne and Godfrey de Bouillon. An inscription translates as 'Good reader, tell me as you pass, which of these men the most valiant was?' The other ceilings are decorated with figures,

*Right: The Chamber of the Nine Worthies at Crathes Castle has a thought-provoking decoration on its beautifully painted ceiling.*

*Below: The staircase at Craigievar Castle was too narrow for a coffin. So although William Forbes entered the castle by door, he finally had to leave by window.*

abstract patterns, moral inscriptions and biblical and poetic quotations. Another fine ceiling, found in the Long Gallery, is panelled in oak and is unique in the whole of Scotland.

### HAUNTED ROOM

The Green Lady's Room at Crathes Castle is so called because it is said to be haunted by the ghost of a young woman dressed in green and carrying a baby in her arms. Legend has it that she was a noble guest at the castle who was made pregnant by a servant. An unfortunate event involving the child may once have taken place in the room, for an infant's skeleton was found by workmen beneath the hearthstone.

### CRAIGIEVAR CASTLE

Near to Crathes Castle, also in Aberdeenshire, stands the handsome six-storey, pink-granite Craigievar Castle. Finished in 1626, it was built in an L-shape by a prosperous merchant named William Forbes, brother of the Bishop of Aberdeen.

William, known as 'Danzig Willie' because he had made his fortune in trading with that port (now known as Gdansk), had purchased the land and half-finished castle in 1610 from the Mortimer family. He poured his wealth into this magnificent romantic castle, which survives virtually unchanged today as another superb example of the Scots tower house.

# LONGLEAT HOUSE
## AND THE CLASSICAL RENAISSANCE

Longleat House in Wiltshire, one of the greatest of the 'prodigy houses', was constructed by Sir John Thynne *c*.1567–80. In 1575, Elizabeth stayed there during her great summer progress.

Thynne, a Shropshire farmer's son, born *c*.1512, had made his name and fortune during the reigns of Henry VIII and Edward VI. He served Edward Seymour, Earl of Hertford, later Duke of Somerset and Lord Protector in Edward VI's boyhood. Thynne was knighted by Somerset on the battlefield at Pinkie, where the Duke's English troops routed a Scots army under the Earl of Arran on 10 September 1547. When Somerset was disgraced and executed, Thynne was cast in the Tower of London for two years and fined £6,000.

The house in which Elizabeth stayed was Thynne's second on the site. He bought the Augustinian Priory at Longleat for £55 in *c*.1540 and began building there in 1546. His first house burned to the ground in 1567, but with typical tenacity he began rebuilding it. The design is Thynne's own, although

*Above: Tudor majesty. Longleat, celebrated as perhaps England's first classical country house, is largely unchanged externally.*

to realize it he employed a number of surveyors, including Frenchman Allan Maynard and Englishman Robert Smythson – the latter subsequently responsible for Hardwick Hall.

Thynne created England's first house in the Italianate, or Renaissance, style. The layout was original: previously most English houses were built around a courtyard, with major rooms looking inwards on to this central space, or in the shape of an 'E', with two end wings

and an entrance porch creating the form of the letter. Thynne, however, built a great cube, with all the major rooms facing outwards towards the surrounding park, and the inner courtyards functioning only to admit light.

### CLASSICAL FAÇADE

Longleat's square outline and decorative elements are derived from classical models. Its façade contains a large number of bay windows, a design inspired by French chateaux, and incorporates the first three classical 'orders'. Beneath the windows are round recesses to hold busts of Roman emperors. Cornices run between the floors, and at roof level there is a balustrade. On the roof are domed turrets intended to be used as intimate banqueting houses. Thynne used the best 'Bath stone' from a quarry at Box, which he bought for the purpose.

### LATER ALTERATIONS

When Elizabeth visited in 1575, only eight years after Thynne had begun rebuilding following the fire, the house stood just two storeys tall. The third level, with Corinthian elements on the façade, was probably added after John Thynne's death, in May 1580, by his son, another John. Since then the exterior of Longleat House has survived largely unchanged, except for elements in the Baroque style that were added in the 1690s, when a doorway was built and four very fine statues were added to the balustrade.

Within the house, most of the rooms were altered in the 19th century; only the magnificent Great Hall survives largely as it was in Thynne's day. This cavernous room is 35ft (11m) high,

*Left: Longleat's interior is much altered. The sweeping Grand Staircase is part of the early 19th-century alterations carried out by Sir Jeffry Wyatville.*

*Above: Beauty well maintained. In 1689, Henry Thynne, brother of Lord Weymouth, wrote that the house's condition was 'so excellent it makes my mouth water'.*

with a vast hammer-beam roof. The elegant carved chimneypiece, Minstrels' Gallery and screen were added around 20 years after Thynne's death, *c.*1600. The Small Gallery dates to 1663, and was built for a visit by Charles II and Queen Catherine just three years after the Restoration. It was Charles II who granted the Thynne family the title of Lord Weymouth. In the years after 1806, most of the other rooms at Longleat were redecorated by Sir Jeffry Wyatville. Further sumptuous redecoration and remodelling was carried out in the 1870s by J.D. Crace.

In the surrounding park, formal gardens were established in the 1690s by George London (d.1714), who also worked at Hampton Court Palace. These were removed by Lawrence 'Capability' Brown, hired in 1757 by the then current Lord Weymouth to landscape the grounds.

### BISHOP KEN'S LIBRARY

Longleat is also famous for its libraries. The family's book and manuscript collection was begun by John Thynne's uncle, William, a clerk in Henry VIII's kitchens. Perhaps surprisingly for one so parsimonious, John Thynne himself greatly expanded it, and by 1577 the collection at Longleat numbered 85 books and manuscripts – a large number for that time. Today, there are eight libraries at Longleat, including the beautiful Bishop Ken's Library, which runs on the top floor along the entire east front of the house. It is named after Thomas Ken, Bishop of Bath and Wells, who was a friend of the Lord Weymouth of his day, and retired to Longleat in 1691 after he was deprived of his bishopric for refusing to swear the required oath of allegiance to William and Mary.

### IN THE MODERN ERA

Longleat House made its mark in the 20th century by becoming, in a blaze of publicity in 1947, the first privately owned stately home to be opened to the paying public. Thereafter, it continued to pioneer new ways of funding its upkeep: in the 1960s, a safari park was opened in the grounds and the house's name became associated with the lions that roam there. Longleat also has a splendid, very challenging 1½ acre (0.6ha) maze, designed by Greg Bright.

### THE THREE 'ORDERS' AT LONGLEAT

Longleat's façade incorporated the first three classical 'orders', or column styles, of ancient Greece and Rome: the Doric, the Ionic and the Corinthian. The house follows the style established by ancient Roman builders of using the columns as decorative features on a façade, running them upwards from ground to roof level: Doric at ground level, Ionic in the middle and Corinthian on the second storey. Longleat is hailed as the first English house to employ the classical orders conspicuously revived in Italy during the Renaissance and advocated in the architectural literature of the 16th century.

*Right: Note the round recesses beneath the windows. These were intended to hold busts of Roman emperors.*

# HARDWICK HALL
## 'MORE GLASS THAN WALL'

 Famously declared to be 'more glass than wall', Hardwick Hall is celebrated above all for its west front, with its glittering array of symmetrically marshalled windows. This bold and overstated exterior conceals many subtle beauties within: its Long Gallery, at 166ft (50.5m) the second longest in Britain, and its elegant High Great Chamber, declared by Sir Sacherevell Sitwell to be 'the most beautiful room, not in England alone, but in the whole of Europe'.

### BESS OF HARDWICK

Hardwick is an enduring monument to the pride and self-belief of its builder, Bess of Hardwick, who rose from fairly humble origins to a position of immense wealth and transcended the architectural fashions of the time to create a highly original house.

Bess, or Elizabeth, was born *c*.1520 to a squire of modest means. She made her first fortune through marriage at the age of 12 to Robert Barlow, a local man only two years older, who died within a few months of the wedding. Around 15 years later, she married Sir William Cavendish,

a very wealthy gentleman who served as Treasurer of the Chamber at the court of Henry VIII. Sir William bought a house at Chatsworth in Derbyshire and rebuilt it in a grand manner befitting his station. His death, in 1557, left Elizabeth hugely wealthy and in possession of several fine properties besides Chatsworth. In 1560, she married Sir William St Loe, Captain of the Queen's Guard, and when he too died, *c*.1565, Bess was wealthier still.

*Above: Elizabeth's family portraits decorate the suitably grand Long Gallery in the East Front. It has an elegant plaster ceiling.*

Her fourth and final marriage, to George Talbot, 6th Earl of Shrewsbury, was her grandest. He too predeceased her, on his death in 1590 leaving an immense inheritance that made Bess one of England's richest women. At the age of 70, Bess, rich enough to leave her mark in some style, set about building Hardwick Hall close to the site of the Old Hall at Hardwick in which she had been born.

This new building, designed to Bess's exacting demands by Robert Smythson, veteran of Longleat House, was built in just six years (1591–7). It was intended to demonstrate in stone and glass how far Bess had risen. Proud of her Shrewsbury title, she had the initials 'ES' ('Elizabeth Shrewsbury') cut beneath a countess's coronet on the house's skyline.

### IMPORTANCE OF SYMMETRY

The house took the form of a three-storey rectangular block, with six four-storey towers arranged around it. It relies for its effect on glass: there is

### EMBROIDERED DECORATION

Even the grandest Elizabethan houses generally had little furniture beyond a few tables, chairs, cupboards and chests for storage. These palaces of the nobility were decorated within using panelling, plasterwork, tapestry and needlework. Hardwick Hall is particularly known for its magnificent embroidery on curtains, wall hangings, cushion covers, upholstery and bedspreads. A fine example is on the bedhead in the State Bedroom.

*Left: The monogram 'ES' for 'Elizabeth Shrewsbury' appears in this embroidered velvet hanging from Hardwick Hall.*

little surface decoration on the house's exterior and the windows have no borders, while the mullions and transoms are kept thin, emphasizing the reflective expanses of window glass. Bess and Smythson put symmetry above all else in the design of the façades; in places, changes in floor level cut across the inside of the great windows.

Within, the two-storey hall is set at an angle of 90 degrees to the main front rather than parallel to it, as was usual with medieval halls. A magnificent, meandering, superbly wide stone staircase leads up to the High Great Chamber. This extraordinary reception room was built to hang eight vast Brussels tapestries, showing the story of wandering Greek hero, Ulysses, that Bess had bought in 1587. They hang beneath a painted plaster frieze representing Diana, the chaste Roman

*Below: Hardwick Hall's famous West Front. Each of the six rooftop pavilions has 'ES' ('Elizabeth Shrewsbury') carved into it.*

hunting goddess, surrounded by animals, nymphs and trees. We know from surviving documents that the beautiful frieze was created by an otherwise unknown craftsman named Charles Williams, who was identified by Bess as a 'cunning plasterer'.

### VAST LONG GALLERY

By the time Bess was building Hardwick Hall, the Long Gallery was a Tudor innovation that had become an essential feature of any great house. It was a kind of indoor promenade, used for the display of portraits and tapestries hung along the gallery walls and for the gentle exercise of guests as they walked up and down the immensely elongated room. At Hardwick, the Long Gallery extends along the entire east front. Lit by 20 tall windows, it is hung with beautiful Flanders tapestries and portraits of Bess, her husbands and children, as well as of various entrepreneurs, including Elizabeth I, Mary, Queen of Scots, the Earl of Leicester and others.

*Above: Hardwick's unusual shape – a long three-storey rectangle with six four-storey towers – can be seen in this aerial view. The house stands in 300 acres (120ha) of park.*

# MAPLEDURHAM HOUSE
## THE REAL TOAD HALL

This handsome Elizabethan country house is the heart of the tiny Oxfordshire village of Mapledurham. It lies near the River Thames and has a remarkably well-preserved working 15th-century water mill on the estate. The house was built in 1588, the year of the Spanish Armada, by Sir Michael Blount, Lieutenant of the Tower of London. It incorporated parts of a 12th-century timber-framed manor house. Sir Michael's grandfather, Richard Blount, had purchased the estate in 1490.

Sir Michael chose warm, rose-red bricks for his house, and his craftsmen achieved attractive patterns in the brickwork. In its essential aspects, the house's

### TOAD HALL?

Kenneth Grahame, author of children's classic *The Wind in the Willows* (1908), lived close to Mapledurham House at Pangbourne and loved the nearby stretch of the River Thames. E.H. Shepard, who provided the famous illustrations for Grahame's book, is believed to have used Mapledurham House as the model for Toad Hall.

*Below: Kenneth Grahame first wrote parts of his book in letters to his partially sighted son, Alistair.*

exterior is unchanged since the Elizabethan era. The Blount family were Roman Catholics, and an interesting feature is the gable decorated with oyster shells at the back of the house – once an accepted signal that a house was a safe refuge for Catholics.

### ALEXANDER POPE

In the early 18th century, poet Alexander Pope, a friend of the Blount sisters, Teresa and Martha, was a frequent visitor to Mapledurham House. Pope played a part in the redesign of the grounds there, introducing William Kent to the family for the commission, which included introducing a 'ha ha' (a sunken boundary, here in the form of a concealed ditch) to create an uninterrupted view of the eastern approach, and to plant a natural-looking 'Pleasure Ground' to the north.

After the Catholic Relief Act of 1791 lifted most of the sanctions against practising Catholics that had been in place since Henry VIII's time, the Blounts built a pretty family chapel in Mapledurham House in 1797. They used the then popular 'Strawberry Hill

*Above: Mapledurham is a fine example of the lesser Elizabethan country house.*

Gothic style', so called after Horace Walpole's house at Twickenham of 1753–78.

Mapledurham originally contained a splendid Great Hall, but this was refashioned as an entrance hall in 1828. By the fireplace are two remarkable wooden deer, carved from a single tree.

*Below: The original 15th-century roof and wall timbers survive amid 17th-century additions in the Mapledurham water mill.*

# LOSELEY PARK
## AND QUEEN ELIZABETH'S PROGRESS

In 1562, leading courtier and trusted royal adviser Sir William More began to rebuild his Surrey manor house at the request of Elizabeth I herself. Like many Tudor landowners, he profited from the Dissolution of the Monasteries, building his 'prodigy house' using blocks of worked stone from the suppressed Cistercian monastery at Waverley Abbey nearby. This stone had first been used 450 years earlier, and must have given his house an established and age-mellowed appearance even when it was newly built.

Sir William constructed a dignified and handsome country house that has survived largely unaltered to the present day. Above the doorway he carved the motto *Invidiae claudor, pateo sed semper amico* ('Envy is barred, but friendship always welcomed'). Elizabeth evidently appreciated Sir William's hospitality and his company, for she visited Loseley House four times. Nor was she the last royal to do so, for James I was a guest of

*Below: Tradition comes to the fore in the handsome Great Hall at Loseley, with its family portraits, antlers and fine furniture.*

*Above: The Holbein fireplace and the gilded ceiling make grand companions in Loseley Park's remarkable Drawing Room.*

Sir George More on two occasions, and many years later, in 1932, Queen Mary also visited Loseley.

### INNER BEAUTIES

The high-ceilinged Great Hall has a splendid oriel window with heraldic glass and Tudor panelling believed to have been removed from Henry VIII's peerless Nonsuch Palace. In the beautiful wood-panelled library, Elizabeth's initials and arms are carved in the overmantel.

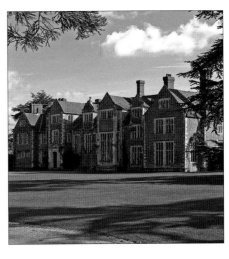

*Above: Loseley Park's name is associated with the dairy products once made from the milk produced by its cows.*

The Drawing Room has a breathtaking and unique fireplace cut from a single block of chalk to a design by Hans Holbein and a superb gilded ceiling that was installed for the visits of James I. In return, James gave the More family a portrait of himself and Queen Anne of Denmark, which can be seen in the Great Hall.

### LATER ALTERATIONS

A new wing was added to Sir William's house *c.*1600, containing a gallery with extra rooms and a riding school. But this wing was demolished in 1820 after it had fallen into a poor condition. Then, in 1877, William More-Molyneux built a nursery wing on the house's south side.

The 21st-century occupants of the house, the More-Molyneuxs, are direct descendants of its 16th-century builder. Their estate of 1,400 acres (565ha) is partly occupied by a celebrated Jersey herd from whose milk the well-known Loseley Jersey ice cream was made. However, the Loseley dairy products are no longer made at the Loseley estate, the brand having been sold to Booker Plc in 1985.

# CAREW CASTLE
## AND THE WELSH COUNTRY HOUSE

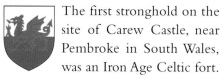

The first stronghold on the site of Carew Castle, near Pembroke in South Wales, was an Iron Age Celtic fort. This was followed by a Norman timber and earthwork stronghold built in 1095 by Gerald de Windsor, a knight who held nearby Pembroke Castle from Henry I. Nothing remains of Gerald's fortress, but part of the east front probably dates from the 12th century. In the inner ward, the Old Tower was added in the early 13th century. A first-floor Great Hall, the Chapel Tower and the South-east Tower were erected in the late 13th century and the gatehouse was built in the early 14th century. This work was carried out by Sir Nicholas de Carew, who also raised a curtain wall to enclose the outer bailey.

### SIR RHYS AP THOMAS

In the late 15th and early 16th centuries, Sir Rhys ap Thomas, an important Welsh ally of Henry VII who had acquired the castle in 1480 from a Carew lord, made

*Below: The solid rooms at Carew Castle were visited by Tudor royalty. Henry VII attended Sir Rhys's grand 1507 celebration.*

*Above: At Carew, the Elizabethan wing (with windows) is to the left; the rounded towers on the right are late 13th century.*

many further improvements, adding a second Great Hall, stairs and splendid accommodation. It was in Carew Castle that Henry Tudor stayed in 1485, while passing through Wales on his way to the Battle of Bosworth, where he won the crown. On the battlefield, Henry knighted Rhys and made him Governor of Wales. In 1507, Sir Rhys threw a lavish celebration at Carew to celebrate the early triumphs of the Tudor dynasty.

### SIR JOHN PERROT

Tudor courtier and statesman 'Good Sir John' Perrot received the lordship and castle of Carew from Queen Mary in 1558, and in 1559, at Elizabeth I's coronation, he was one of the four bearers of her 'canopy of state'. He rose to high position under Elizabeth, who granted him governorship of Carew, serving the Queen first as Lord of Munster and then as Lord Deputy of Ireland. He added a

*Below: This interior view of steep steps and low doorways at Carew gives a sense of what life was like within a medieval or Tudor castle.*

## BACHECRAIG

The Tudor country mansion of Bachecraig near Denbigh is celebrated as the first classical house in Wales. It was built in the early part of Elizabeth's reign by the immensely wealthy Sir Richard Clough (d.1570). It was constructed on a grand scale, with continental ideas of proportion very much in mind: the chimneys, as well as the windows and other features, are carefully balanced for symmetry. Local legend has it that Sir Richard made a midnight pact with the Devil to supply the bricks he used for his house – and that these were fashioned from local clay, fired in an infernal kiln and supplied each morning, one day's worth at a time. Scholars believe that Sir Richard gained a reputation for dubious night-time work because he kept an astronomical observatory in the roof of Bachecraig and was often seen to be labouring there at night.

*Above: Laugharne Castle occupies a cliff, the site of a Norman ringwork, looking out across the estuary of the River Taf.*

magnificent three-storey wing containing a majestic second-floor Long Gallery that ran for 130ft (40m). In its impressive, typically Elizabethan façade were two rows of big rectangular windows as well as two large oriel windows. Like the rest of this once-proud castle, it is now a sad ruin.

A man of fiery temper known for his 'majesty of personage', Perrot was rumoured at court to be an illegitimate son of Henry VIII, and, judging from his portraits, he certainly looked like the King. But his proud manner made him many enemies and he was convicted of high treason in 1591, before dying of natural causes the following year during imprisonment in the Tower of London.

### LAUGHARNE AND POWIS

'Good Sir John' also refashioned and rebuilt the castle at Laugharne, in South Wales, into an Elizabethan country mansion after he was given the fortress by Elizabeth I in 1575. However, his

work there apparently fell to ruin within a few years of his death in 1592, and most of what is visible today at Laugharne dates from the castle's earlier history.

### A COUNTRY HOUSE CASTLE

Powis Castle in central Wales was another military stronghold upgraded to become a fine Elizabethan country house. This attractive battlemented building, celebrated above all for its magnificent terraced gardens, has seen many refurbishments, most recently in the early 20th century. In the Tudor era, Sir Edward Herbert, who gained ownership of Powis in 1578 and whose family still live there, undertook extensive rebuilding and modernization work in 1587–95. All that survives today is the Long Gallery, although the castle still has several rooms with Elizabethan furnishings.

*Below: Powis Castle stands on a commanding hilltop, its steep south-east approaches today occupied by gardens.*

# MONTACUTE HOUSE
## AND WOLLATON HALL

In the 1590s, Somerset landowner Sir Edward Phelips began building Montacute House from beautiful honey-coloured limestone quarried at nearby Ham Hill. He employed a gifted Somerset master mason, William Arnold, who must take a great deal of the credit for Montacute, and who later worked at Cranbourne Manor in Dorset for Robert Cecil, 1st Earl of Salisbury.

*Below: The end of the east front at Montacute House, with its curved Flemish gables, slender chimneys and large windows.*

*Above: The salvaged archway from Clifton Maybank makes a grand entrance in the centre of the west front at Montacute House.*

Sir Edward needed a house grand enough to match his position, for he was a leading lawyer and politician in London. An MP from 1584, he was elected Speaker of the House of Commons in 1604. As a lawyer, he made the opening speech for the prosecution at the trial of Guy Fawkes after the discovery of the 'Gunpowder Plot' to blow up the Houses of Parliament in 1605.

### THE ENTRANCE FRONT

With William Arnold, Phelips created a remarkable east entrance front at Montacute. The façade, 90ft (27m) high and almost 200ft (60m) across, is another Elizabethan 'wall of glass': it contains 39 mullioned windows, arranged in three perfectly symmetrical tiers. These straight horizontal lines are brought to life by the curves of the Flemish gables, the vertical lines of the slender chimneys on the roof above and a wealth of carved detail in the façade itself, including curved cornices on some of the windows and circular recesses that probably once held terra-cotta medallions. A delightful touch is

*Above: An oak bedstead at Montacute is carved with the arms of James I and of Frederick V, Elector Palatine of the Rhine.*

## WOLLATON HALL, NOTTINGHAMSHIRE

The great Elizabethan surveyor Robert Smythson, who worked at Longleat House as well as Hardwick Hall, built the ravishing Wollaton Hall in Nottinghamshire for Sir Francis Willoughby in 1580–88. He used Italian

master masons and probably worked to the designs of celebrated artist John Thorpe, based on those of Sir Francis himself. This elegant 'prodigy house' is highly ornamented: the four large corner towers are topped with pinnacles and the façades incorporate niches filled with the busts of great philosophers. In the centre of the house, the hall is elevated above the surrounding wings. Wollaton Hall is reputed to have cost the astonishing sum of £80,000 to build.

*Left: At Wollaton Hall the central hall rises above the rest of the house; its four square corner towers rise to pinnacles.*

---

the inclusion between the windows of the top storey of statues representing the 'Nine Worthies', here in the guise of Roman centurions. All the detail is in the same rich-coloured Ham Hill limestone as the main house.

A grass forecourt with side flowerbeds extends before the east front and is enclosed by a low wall. Two delicate corner pavilions have domed roofs and oriel windows on all four sides. Originally, a grand gatehouse stood in the centre of the front wall between the two pavilions, but it has been demolished.

Montacute contains the longest of all Elizabethan Long Galleries: the top-floor 'promenade' runs 172ft (52m) along the entire length of the house, and is 20ft (6m) across. Groups of connected rooms lead off either end of the gallery. Today it houses a splendid selection of 100 Tudor and Jacobean portraits from the collection of the National Portrait Gallery in London.

Aside from the Long Gallery, Montacute's finest room is certainly the Library, originally the Great Chamber. The panes of heraldic glass in the windows, the chimney-piece of Portland stone, a fine plasterwork frieze and the beautiful 16th-century wood panelling on the walls are all original.

### WEST FRONT AND GARDENS
In 1786–7, Edward Phelips changed the entrance front to the west side. He salvaged a beautiful stone porch from a Tudor house at Clifton Maybank in Somerset that was being pulled down, and had it fitted into the centre of the front. The porch is made from the same stone as Montacute, and although it was made around 50 years before Montacute, its detail fits its new setting perfectly.

Ornamental gardens with elegant lines of yew trees lie to the north and south ends of the house. In the forecourt on the east front (the original entrance), are two flowerbeds planted in the 1950s to designs by Vita Sackville-West, poet, novelist and gardener.

*Below: A late 19th-century watercolour shows one of the graceful domed pavilions in Montacute's formal east garden.*

# CHAPTER THREE

# THE JACOBEAN COUNTRY HOUSE

## *c.*1600–*c.*1650

In 1616, Inigo Jones, recently appointed Surveyor of Works to King James I, began work on the Queen's House in Greenwich for James's wife, Anne of Denmark. Jones had recently returned from a visit to Rome, during which he had studied ancient Roman buildings and the work of Italian Renaissance architects, including Andrea Palladio and Vincenzo Scamozzi. Jones introduced 'classical' architectural design – inspired by Renaissance and ancient Roman buildings – into England.

As well as being England's first classical architect, he was a major influence on the 'Palladian' movement of the 18th century, in which architects returned to Palladio as a source of inspiration.

The elegant Queen's House was abandoned when Anne died in 1619 and only finished in 1635 for Charles II's queen, Henrietta Maria.

In the mean time, Inigo Jones had designed and built the magnificent Banqueting House in the royal palace of Whitehall and the Queen's Chapel, St James's, and worked on or supervised country houses at New Hall, Essex, Stoke Bruerne, Northamptonshire, and Chevening, Kent.

The career of Inigo Jones was a turning point in English architecture: the domestic tradition had come to a final flowering with acclaimed Jacobean houses such as Hatfield House, built in 1608–11; in contrast, the superb south front built in 1636–40 at Wilton House, Wiltshire, designed under Jones's supervision, showed a new way forward. It used a classical design, with devices such as the central window with carved figures that were taken directly from Jones's royal buildings in London, inspired in their turn by the designs of Scamozzi in Rome.

*Left: Paintings by Sir Peter Paul Rubens were fitted in 1635 into the beamed ceiling of Inigo Jones's superb Banqueting House, Whitehall, completed in 1622.*

# KNOLE
## HOME OF VITA SACKVILLE-WEST

The vast and historic country house of Knole, Sevenoaks, in Kent, was largely created by two men – Thomas Bourchier, a 15th-century Archbishop of Canterbury, and Thomas Sackville, 1st Earl of Dorset – in the early reign of King James I. This palatial house of grey Kentish ragstone with brown roof-tiles, so extensive that from a distance it resembles a village or small town, has remained largely unaltered since the sensitive external alterations and large-scale internal reworking carried out by Thomas Sackville around 400 years ago.

Sackville descendants have lived in Knole for over 400 years, and still inhabit part of the mansion today, although the house has been owned, managed and maintained by the National Trust since 1946.

*Below: Knole's beautiful staircase, installed by Thomas Sackville, leads up to the equally grand Ballroom. Note the Sackville leopard atop the newel post (right).*

---

### HOUSE OF POETS

Thomas Sackville (1536–1608) was a poet and dramatist in his youth before settling into political life, and he co-wrote with Thomas Norton the first tragic play in English, *Gorboduc* or *Ferrex and Porrex*. The play, which describes conflicts among legendary rulers of ancient Britain, was performed on Twelfth Night 1561 in the Inner Temple Hall, London. Over the centuries, Sackville's house had many admirers. Edmund Burke declared it 'the most interesting thing in England'. Vita Sackville West (1892–1962) was born and lived there before her marriage to Harold Nicholson. Her sometime lover

*Right: Vita Sackville West loved the colours of Knole. She wrote, "It is above all an English home ... It has the tone of England; it melts into the green of the garden turf."*

and close friend Virginia Woolf used Knole as the setting for her novel *Orlando* (1928). Vita herself used the house as the setting for a novel, *The Edwardians* (1930), and wrote a book about the house, *Knole and the Sackvilles*, published in 1922.

---

### MEDIEVAL AND TUDOR PALACE

Thomas Bourchier bought the estate at Knole with its 13th-century house in 1456 for £266. Over the next three decades, he reconstructed and extended it into a grand episcopal palace with seven interconnecting courtyards, including two extensive quadrangles – the Stone Court and the Green Court – which stand one in front of the other at the entrance. In line with 15th-century practice, his house made at least a show of fortification, with extensive battlements on walls and towers, as well as two gatehouses. On the inner gate-house, known as 'Bourchier's Tower', there is decorative machicolation.

Knole was the palace of five arch-bishops of Canterbury, from Thomas Bourchier to Thomas Cranmer. After Cranmer it passed to King Henry VIII in 1538, and was a royal palace for 28 years until Elizabeth I gave it to

Thomas Sackville in 1566. The house was on lease until the year of Elizabeth's death, and so Sackville did not start his work on Knole until 1603, when he transformed the interior and made a series of well-judged alterations to the outer fabric that greatly accentuated its overall attractiveness.

### SACKVILLE'S ALTERATIONS

To soften the house's fortress-like appearance, Thomas Sackville added mullioned windows and curved gables in the Flemish style, with decorative finials in the likeness of the leopards from the Sackville crest. In the Stone Court, he built a fine colonnade with a gallery above it.

Internally, he remodelled the Great Hall of 1460, adding a lower, plastered ceiling and a sumptuously carved oak screen. He added a beautiful timber Great Staircase, painted by artist Paul

*Above: A great part of Knole's appeal lies in the fact that its exterior today looks largely as it did in the time of King James I.*

Isaacson in yellows and greens, with a number of visual effects, including *trompe l'oeil* images of the balustrade on the walls, which were startlingly original at the time. The staircase, which has Sackville leopards above its newel posts, led to the Ballroom, where Sackville installed an extraordinary alabaster and marble chimney-piece and over-mantel made by Cornelius Cuer, royal master mason. This extravagantly grand room, which also features glorious painted oak panelling depicting mermaids and mermen, served as a reception chamber and dining room.

Sackville also built three grand galleries, including the Cartoon Gallery, with another splendid Jacobean ceiling and chimney-piece. The gallery takes it name from the copies of Raphael's cartoons (designs for paintings) made by artist Daniel Mytens, who was court painter to Charles I.

The cycles of time take solid form in this outstanding house. In addition to seven courtyards, for the days of the

*Right: Thomas Sackville built the Cartoon Gallery in the 1600s, but the six copies of Raphael's cartoons were fitted in 1701.*

week, there are said to be 52 staircases, for the weeks of the year, and 365 rooms, for the days of the year. Many have commented on Knole's very English beauty and atmosphere. The poet and novelist Vita Sackville West, who grew up there, said Knole had 'a deep inward gaiety' and likened the house to 'some very old woman who has always been beautiful, who has had many lovers and seen many generations come and go … and learnt an imperishable secret of tolerance and humour'.

## LATER CHANGES

Since Thomas Sackville's changes, there have been some alterations to the house's furnishings and its decorative schemes, although the prevailing style remains Tudor and Jacobean. In the late 17th century, Thomas's great-great-grandson, Charles, 6th Earl of Dorset, added fine furniture and textiles. Then, around a century later, John Frederick, 3rd Duke of Dorset, installed many Old Masters that he had purchased during a Grand Tour of continental Europe.

# HATFIELD HOUSE
## HOME OF THE CECIL FAMILY

Robert Cecil, 1st Earl of Salisbury, had little choice when King James I 'suggested' that they swap houses. James would take for himself the beautiful Theobalds in Hertfordshire, built by Robert's father, William Cecil, Lord Burghley, and would give Robert the nearby royal palace of Hatfield.

The Tudor palace at Hatfield was built *c.*1485 by Cardinal John Morton, Bishop of Ely and later Archbishop of Canterbury under King Henry VII. Henry VIII seized it and used it mainly as a home, often effectively a prison, for his children. The future Elizabeth I spent most of her childhood at Hatfield, where she was told the news that her elder sister, Mary, had died, making her Queen of England. In her first act as Queen, Elizabeth appointed William Cecil her Principal Secretary, then held her first Council meeting in Hatfield's Great Hall.

The tower and Great Hall of the 15th-century palace are all that survive, for in 1607–08 Robert Cecil pulled

*Below: A new direction? The tower, arcade, gables and forecourt point forward to the classical architecture of Inigo Jones – some say Jones himself designed the arcade.*

down three sides of the original building as he set about constructing a new residence, devising his own floor plans and designs.

### ROYAL VISITORS

Like Burghley House and the other great 'prodigy houses' of the Elizabethan reign, Hatfield was designed to be a fitting venue for entertaining the monarch. A central block contained the main staterooms used for receiving and entertaining guests: there was a Great Hall in the centre, with a Long Gallery and four great rooms on the upper floor; the chapel stood at the side. This central building was flanked by two wings containing apartments for royal visitors: the queen in the west wing and the king on the east side. Terraced gardens were laid out complete with a lake and fountains, and with rare plants and trees imported from continental Europe by the botanist John Tradescant.

The house was completed in four years (1607–11), but Robert Cecil died the following year. In later years, his house was often visited by kings and queens, including James I, Charles I, James, Duke of York (the future James II) and Queen Victoria and Prince Albert.

*Above: Among the many treasures at Hatfield is this genealogical chart that purports to trace Elizabeth I's descent from Adam.*

### CONTRASTING STYLES

The north and south front are in contrasting styles. The north front, of red brick with symmetrical lines of wide windows, providing an essentially flat surface varied by shallow bays, appears to be in a familiar domestic 'Tudor' style. The south front, however, has two projecting wings forming a forecourt,

an elegant arcade in the Italian style, a delicate white tower and Flemish gables. Cecil's surveyor was Robert Lyminge and the master mason a certain Conn; Inigo Jones may have contributed to the stone forecourt on the south front. French, English and Flemish craftsmen were hired. They used bricks from the demolished wings of the Tudor palace, stone from Caen in Normandy and the finest marble from Carrara in Tuscany.

## PORTRAITS OF A QUEEN

Hatfield House contains two of the most celebrated portraits of Elizabeth I. The first is the 'Ermine Portrait' by Nicholas Hilliard, so called because an ermine (an animal symbolic of royalty) is portrayed with the Queen; this hangs in the Marble Hall. The second is the 'Rainbow Portrait', probably by Hilliard's pupil, Isaac Oliver, but sometimes attributed to Marcus Gheeraerts the Younger. This is a veritable riot of symbolism, in which Elizabeth is shown wearing a gown embroidered with English wildflowers and holding a rainbow, symbolic of peace.

*Below: The 'Rainbow Portrait' of Queen Elizabeth I.*

Hatfield House contains two splendid examples of Jacobean style at its most flamboyant: the Grand Staircase, which is fitted with 'dog gates' to prevent animals going up, and is made of intricately carved oak, and the exuberantly decorated Marble Hall, which is often identified by architectural historians as the last great medieval hall in an English house. Also of note is the beautiful original stained glass, depicting Old Testament scenes, fitted in the chapel in 1609.

### PROMINENT CECILS

Hatfield House has remained through the centuries in the hands of the Cecils, who, in the late 19th century, rose once again to great prominence – Robert Arthur Talbot Gascoyne-Cecil, 3rd Marquess of Salisbury, was leader of the Conservative Party and three times Prime Minister.

*Below: The gardens at Hatfield House were restored in the Victorian era. They include herb gardens and orchards as well as terraces.*

# BOLSOVER CASTLE
## SMYTHSON'S LAST HOUSE

 Bolsover Castle, near Chesterfield in Derbyshire, was the last major house designed by the leading surveyor of the Elizabethan age, Robert Smythson. He began work at Bolsover for Sir Charles Cavendish in 1612.

The first castle on the site, a stone keep with a curtain wall, had been built by William Peverel (an illegitimate son of William the Conqueror) in the 12th century. But it was little more than a ruin by the mid-16th century, when it was bought by George Talbot, 6th Earl of Shrewsbury and fourth husband of Bess of Hardwick. He leased the castle in 1608 to his stepson, Sir Charles Cavendish. Sir Charles bought the house in 1613.

### A FANTASY CASTLE
Sir Charles Cavendish and Robert Smythson built a delightful fantasy castle, an embodiment of Elizabethan-Jacobean ideals of chivalry. The tower keep,

*Below: Bolsover Castle occupies a hilltop and commands fine views of the countryside – especially from the Terrace Range.*

completed after Smythson's death in 1621, is today called 'the little castle'. It contains a series of elaborately decorated panelled rooms, with allegorical wall paintings and magnificent marble fireplaces. These rooms include the famous Star Chamber, Pillar Chamber, Elysium Chamber and Heaven Chamber. It gives on to a court with a central fountain (the Fountain Court). Tower and court occupy the site of William Peverel's original keep and inner bailey, and some parts of the walls of the Fountain Court are medieval originals.

The staterooms were in the Terrace Range, designed by Smythson and his son John, and included a Great Hall, very fine living quarters and a splendid 220ft (67m) Long Gallery. The Riding School range, designed by Robert Smythson's grandson, Huntingdon, has a superb timber roof of the early 1630s.

### NEW OWNERS
In the Civil War, its owner, Sir William Cavendish, led the Royalist army at Marston Moor and following that defeat fled into exile. The castle was occupied by the Parliamentarians, but

### ROBERT SMYTHSON
In a series of major building commissions between 1556 and his death in 1614, Robert Smythson achieved a creative blend of native English, Flemish and continental Renaissance architectural ideas. Although he was a figure of major significance for Elizabethan and Jacobean architecture, he lived before practitioners of his trade could claim great social standing. There is no surviving image of him, and we know little about him beyond the building projects on which he worked. His first house was Longleat for Sir John Thynne, begun when he was just 21. He was later surveyor on those jewels of the age, Hardwick Hall and Wollaton Hall.

Sir William returned after 1660. Subsequently, the castle passed through the hands of various owners and residents until it was given to the state in 1945 by William Cavendish-Bentinck, 7th Duke of Portland. English Heritage is currently responsible for the castle.

# DUNFERMLINE PALACE
## AND GLAMIS CASTLE

Before he became King of England, James Stuart, ruling as James VI of Scotland, established a fine royal palace at Dunfermline. The main part of the palace was originally a guesthouse in the Benedictine abbey founded by Queen Margaret and her son, David I; James also added a new building at Dunfermline, the Queen's House, for his wife, Anne of Denmark.

Royal connections to Dunfermline were well established. Queen (later Saint) Margaret was buried there, as was Robert I the Bruce, who had rebuilt the abbey's domestic buildings after they were ransacked by the army of Edward I of England. James I was born at the abbey, and James IV and James V stayed there.

James VI's palace was built around a courtyard, with the main range of royal apartments at the south-west, the new Queen's House to the north and the abbey buildings to the east. The main range incorporated parts of the medieval abbey guesthouse. The palace was the birthplace of Prince Charles (the future King Charles I, and the last monarch born in Scotland) in 1600. The palace is a ruin today, with only part of the outer shell of the south-west range surviving.

*Below: The remains of the south-west range at Dunfermline Palace. It once contained a large hall, with a kitchen and chamber.*

### GLAMIS CASTLE

The magnificent Banqueting Hall at Glamis Castle was built in the early 1600s as part of a substantial reworking of this largely 15th-century fortress by Patrick Lyon, the 9th Lord Glamis and 1st Earl of Kinghorne. The castle stands on the site of a building in which King Malcolm II was reputedly murdered; it was then a royal hunting lodge for many years and was the home of Janet Douglas, Lady Glamis, who was imprisoned and

*Above: Glamis Castle. The impressive main tower was constructed c. 1435. The oldest part is the east wing, built c. 1400.*

then burned at the stake as a witch. James V briefly seized the castle for four years. Mary, Queen of Scots, visited, and James VI came to stay often. In the 20th century, it was the childhood home of Queen Elizabeth, the Queen Mother; in 1930, she gave birth there to Princess Margaret, sister of Queen Elizabeth II.

# AUDLEY END
## A PALACE IN ALL BUT NAME

The country mansion of Audley End, near Saffron Walden, was built by Thomas Howard, 1st Earl of Suffolk, in 1605–14 to entertain King James I. Before its 18th-century alterations, it was more than twice the size it is today. Howard served as Lord Treasurer to the King and perhaps gave in to the temptation to divert funds towards the building of his house, for in 1619 he and his wife were imprisoned in the Tower of London, accused of embezzling thousands of pounds.

To create the grandest home in England of its day, Thomas Howard demolished an earlier house, Audley Inn, which had been erected by his grandfather, Sir Thomas Audley, in the middle of the 16th century. Sir Thomas himself had built on the site of a former Benedictine monastery, named Walden Abbey, given to him by Henry VIII in 1538 during the Dissolution of the Monasteries.

*Below: The Great Hall. Note the Howard family crests in the plaster ceiling and the superb Jacobean carved wooden screen.*

The new house, Audley End, built around two courtyards, has two porches on the front with separate entrances that led to separate suites of apartments for the king and queen. Within, the splendid Great Hall features a magnificent Jacobean carved oak screen, while the plaster panel ceiling is decorated with coloured crests of the Howard family.

Thomas Howard was rewarded with only one visit from James I, in 1614. James supposedly told his host: 'the building is too large for a King, but it might do for a Lord Treasurer'. In fact, Audley End became a royal palace between 1668 and 1701, when Charles II

*Above: Audley End, built to impress James I, became a palace when Charles II bought it as a base from which to attend horse-racing at Newmarket.*

purchased it for the sum of £50,000 (it was repurchased by the earls of Suffolk). He stayed there in style and comfort when attending horse-racing at nearby Newmarket.

### FORMAL GARDENS
Thomas Howard created vast, elaborate gardens with extended avenues of trees, and geometric arrangements of alleys and rectangular ponds. These designs led the eye along a main vista from the house's principal front, with another, lesser, vista at right angles.

### FASHIONABLE ALTERATIONS
In the 18th century, after many decades of neglect, Sir John Griffin Griffin, 1st Baron Braybrooke, and a descendant of the earls of Suffolk, abandoned these gardens and hired Lancelot 'Capability' Brown to remake the grounds in the then fashionable landscape style. He also engaged Robert Adam to create a fine set of eight rooms, squeezed into the lower ground floor, refit the saloon, create a picture gallery, redecorate the chapel and build a number of garden monuments, including the Tea House Bridge that crosses the River Cam.

# BLICKLING HALL
## A JACOBEAN MANSION

Robert Lyminge, surveyor-architect for Sir Robert Cecil at Hatfield House, built the Jacobean mansion of Blickling Hall in Norfolk in 1616–25 for Sir Henry Hobart, Lord Chief Justice under King James I. Blickling's delightful entrance front uses many of the features of Hatfield, including a large clock tower, a prominent and decorated porch and ogival cupolas at the corners.

The new house was built on the site of an older Blickling Hall that had once belonged to Sir Thomas Boleyn, father of Anne Boleyn, queen of Henry VIII and mother of Elizabeth I. Unlike Hatfield House, Blicking Hall was constrained by its setting – indeed the yew hedges and the former moat (now a flower garden) are a good deal older than the Jacobean house. Perhaps because of these constraints, Lyminge decided to build a conventional courtyard house rather than adopt the fashionable H-shape used at Hatfield.

*Below: The Long Gallery has been used as a library since the 18th century. Today it houses a collection of rare books.*

*Above: This detail of a musician is from the plaster ceiling of the Long Gallery.*

### HALL AND LONG GALLERY

The main entrance hall contains the majestic original Jacobean oak staircase, which was moved and extended when the hall was rebuilt in 1767 by a local architect, Thomas Ivory. His staircase splits into two at the main landing, while the original had one flight only, but the reconstruction is a work of great skill.

Blickling Hall's Long Gallery was one of the last but also one of the finest long galleries built in an English country house.

It is 123ft (37m) long, and fills most of the house's east front. The room is a good deal wider than most long galleries, and has a magnificent plaster ceiling full of abstract and naturalistic designs, which was carved by Edward Stanyan in 1620. It houses a library of 12,000 volumes.

*Below: The clock tower and ogival cupolas at the corners are among the features at Blickling Hall that recall Hatfield House.*

# THE QUEEN'S HOUSE, GREENWICH
## 'HOUSE OF DELIGHT'

 Artist-turned-architect Inigo Jones's first major commission, after being appointed Surveyor of Works to King James I in 1615, was to design the Queen's House in Greenwich for James's wife, Anne of Denmark. Anne died in 1619, before the Queen's House was complete, but Jones returned to finish the work in 1635 at the request of King Charles I's wife, Henrietta Maria of France.

When Jones built the Queen's House it was part of the 15th-century royal palace of Placentia, birthplace both of Henry VIII (in 1491) and Elizabeth I (in 1533). This palace and its estate stood on the large riverside site now occupied by Greenwich Park, the National Maritime Museum and the Royal Naval College. Following the Restoration of the monarchy in 1660, Charles II set out to rebuild the Palace of Placentia to the designs of John Webb, an architect who, with Inigo Jones, pioneered the

classical style in England. The only part of Webb's work that survives today is the east range of the King Charles block; the rest has been demolished.

### ITALIAN INSPIRATION
Jones's design for the Queen's House was based on that of an Italian villa at Poggio a Caiano, built for Florentine statesman Lorenzo de Medici and completed in 1485 by Giuliano da Sangallo. Like Poggio a Caiano, the Queen's House consists of two main parts: one part stood within Placentia Palace and the second was in Greenwich Park, and they were connected by a covered bridge over the public road (moved in 1699 by Lord Romney, Ranger of the Royal Park) linking Deptford and Woolwich. Other key elements of the design derived from Jones's Italian model are the curved steps, terrace and widely spaced windows on the palace side of the building (the north front) and the open colonnade of six Ionic pillars along the park face (the south front). From the colonnade, which Jones called 'a frontispiece in the midst', there is a splendid view of the parkland.

*Above: An Italian villa in Greenwich. The south front, with its colonnade of Ionic pillars, commands superb views of the park.*

### FIRST OF JONES'S CUBES
Jones designed all the interiors. There were elaborate marble fireplaces and the rooms were adorned with carved wooden friezes. In the palace, or north, building he created a magnificent entrance hall, paved with black and white marble, its dimensions a perfect 40ft (12m) cube. This was the first of several cubes built by Jones – two side by side (a 'double cube') were used both in the Whitehall Palace Banqueting House and in the rebuilt south wing at Wilton House. In favouring these perfect dimensions, Jones was following one of the key tenets of Palladio, that houses should be designed in line with natural laws of symmetry, proportion and harmony. His entrance hall in the Queen's House was also the first instance in an English house of a hall designed for use as a reception room. Its ceiling was decorated with paintings by Orazio Gentileschi, representing the 'Arts of Peace'.

---

### QUEEN'S CHAPEL, ST JAMES'S
Inigo Jones received the royal order to build the Queen's Chapel at St James's Palace in April 1623. It was planned as a Roman Catholic place of worship in which the intended wife of Charles, Prince of Wales, could hear Mass. Charles travelled to Spain with the Duke of Buckingham to woo the Infanta but failed in the mission, returning home empty-handed in October 1623. Instead, the chapel was used by Charles's eventual queen, Henrietta Maria of France, also a Roman Catholic. It is in the form of a double cube, with a gracefully curving coffered ceiling and at the east end an elegant arched three-light Venetian window – a much-used device in the Palladian revival.

*Above: From the river side, the neat Queen's House is dwarfed by Sir Christopher Wren's Royal Naval Hospital.*

### THE 'HOUSE OF DELIGHT'

Jones also installed England's first open-well spiral staircase, the Tulip Staircase, bringing all his delicacy to bear when

*Below: This ceiling of the Arts and Sciences (1636) was painted for the Queen's House but later moved to Marlborough House.*

he designed a balustrade of wrought iron decorated with the fleur-de-lys device as a mark of respect for the French-born queen. In the Queen's Drawing Room there hung a fine tapestry of Cupid and Psyche by Jacob Jordaens, perhaps after which she called the building her 'House of Delight'.

After the Restoration, when Henrietta Maria, now the Queen Mother, returned to live there, the Queen's House was enlarged by John Webb as part of Charles II's large-scale plan to rebuild Placentia Palace. Nearby, Charles's new palace, the King's House, was begun on land beside the River Thames. It was never finished and later became the site of the Royal Naval Hospital, designed by Sir Christopher Wren.

### STOKE PARK PAVILIONS

At Stoke Bruerne, Northamptonshire, Inigo Jones either designed or supervised the design of a country house for Sir Francis Crane. The house was never completed, and large parts were burned down in 1886, but two pavilions and colonnades have survived and can be seen today. The plan, with the

central house connected to two pavilions by a graceful curving colonnade, was based on that of the mid-16th-century Villa di Papa Giulio in Rome, built by Giacomo Barozzi da Vignola for Pope Julius II. At Stoke Bruerne, the west pavilion contained a library and the east pavilion a chapel.

*Below: One of two graceful pavilions designed by Jones for Sir Francis Crane's country house at Stoke Bruerne, Northants.*

# THE BANQUETING HOUSE, WHITEHALL
## A MASTERPIECE OF CLASSICAL ARCHITECTURE

When King James I's Banqueting Hall in Whitehall Palace burned down in 1619 he commanded his Surveyor of Works, Inigo Jones, to replace it. Jones's Banqueting House, completed in three years by 1622, is his masterpiece. One of England's first and greatest classical buildings, it is the only part of the once extensive royal palace of Whitehall to survive today above ground. Contemporaries, however, seem to have found Jones's conception too grand and rather at odds with the rest of the Tudor palace. One response, in 1621, was that the hall was 'too faire and nothing suitable to the rest of the house'.

### IONIC AND CORINTHIAN

The Banqueting House was designed not for dining but principally as a setting for state occasions, plays and the masques that Inigo Jones continued to design for the royal court. Indeed, its completion was celebrated with the performance of *The Masque of Augurs*, by Jones and

*Below: The Banqueting House survived in its original setting – as part of Whitehall Palace – for only 76 years, from completion in 1622 to the disastrous fire of 1698.*

Ben Jonson, on Twelfth Night 1622. The building's interior was Jones's version of a Roman basilica (hall): it consists of a vast 50ft (15m) double cube, and is ornamented with Ionic columns beneath a cantilevered gallery and Corinthian pilasters above.

This formidable interior space originally had a beamed ceiling, but the celebrated painted panels by Sir Peter Paul Rubens were fitted in 1635. The paintings are allegorical representations of James I's reign as a time of

*Above: Work of a master – Inigo Jones's Banqueting House façade facing Whitehall. Architects praise its vitality and harmony.*

plenty and peace; Rubens had planned them at the time of building, but they were not finished until 1634.

Jones' façade for the Banqueting House also uses Ionic beneath Corinthian pilasters. Facing Whitehall, it was originally built using three colours of stone: brown for the basement, a dun colour for the upper walls and white Portland

## INIGO JONES: CLASSICAL PIONEER

The son of a London cloth worker, Inigo Jones first found royal employment as a painter at the court of Christian IV of Denmark and Norway. His work there gained him an entrée at the royal court in London, where he served Queen Anne (Christian IV's sister) from 1605 onward as a designer of costumes, scenery and effects for royal entertainments, or 'masques'. His first architectural work, commissioned by Robert Cecil, 1st Earl of Salisbury, was a design for the New Exchange in the Strand, London (demolished in the 18th century). Jones was then appointed Surveyor of Works, first to Henry, Prince of Wales, in 1610–12, and in 1615–43 to Kings James I and Charles I.

*Above: Jones was a superb theatrical designer and one of England's greatest architects.*

An admirer of classical Roman and Italian Renaissance architecture, Jones pioneered 'classicism' in English architecture, basing his designs on those of the Roman architect Vitrivius and his Italian followers Andrea Palladio and Vincenzo Scamozzi, and on study of Vitrivius's and Palladio's writings on architecture.

In addition to his major royal buildings in London, Jones contributed to the design and interior decoration of a number of country houses. He also designed and laid out London's first integrated square at Covent Garden and restored the old St Paul's Cathedral, though his reputedly superb work there was entirely lost in the Great Fire of London in 1666.

---

stone for the columns and the elegant balustrade. But it was refaced with Portland stone throughout during restoration by Sir John Soane in 1829.

### WHITEHALL PALACE

In the 15th century, the Archbishops of York built as their London base a palace named York Place, which stood on the site of Inigo Jones's Banqueting House. When Cardinal Thomas Wolsey became Archbishop of York in 1514, he extended the palace, which, like Hampton Court, another of Wolsey's splendid residences, attracted the covetous eye of Henry VIII. In the late 1520s, his reputation failing and desperately trying to retain the King's favour, Wolsey gave York Place to Henry. Renamed Whitehall Palace it became Henry VIII's principal royal residence.

The King further extended and improved it, rebuilding a fine Privy Gallery that he had taken from another of Wolsey's houses, at Esher. He built a

*Right: Roman basilica updated – the great double cube of the Banqueting Hall. Note the Ionic columns beneath and the Corinthian pilasters above the gallery.*

bowling alley, a tilt yard, a cockpit and real tennis courts and raised two great gateways over the roadway (from Charing Cross to Westminster) that ran through the palace complex. Within the many rooms of the palace, several walls and ceilings were painted by Hans Holbein, court painter from 1536.

The palace was later a favourite of Elizabeth I, although she made few alterations, and of Charles I. Most of this vast palace, which was said to contain 2,000 rooms, burned down in a single night in 1698 during the reign of William III and Mary II. Only Jones's Banqueting House was spared.

# WILTON HOUSE
## SEAT OF THE EARLS OF PEMBROKE

In the late 1630s, Philip Herbert, 4th Earl of Pembroke, built a magnificent new south front to his family's Tudor mansion at Wilton House in Wiltshire. Construction, carried out by the Frenchman Isaac de Caus, was supervised and directed by Inigo Jones, who designed seven magnificent staterooms for the interior.

The original Wilton House was built by Sir William Herbert on land that formerly belonged to Wilton Abbey, which he was given by King Henry VIII in 1544. Sir William was related to the King by marriage, as his first wife, Anne, was the sister of Henry's sixth wife, Catherine Parr. In 1551, Henry made Sir William 1st Earl of Pembroke. At Wilton, Sir William built a fine courtyard house in the second half of the 1540s. The commanding tower in the centre of Wilton's east front is a survival from his splendid house.

### WILTON'S SOUTH FRONT
The new south front of the 1630s was originally intended as the right half of a much longer façade, which was to have had a portico with six Corinthian

*Below: In de Caus's original design, the south front as we see it was just the right half of a longer façade with a central portico.*

*Above: The east front (right) and the south front (left) at Wilton. The sedate exterior gives no hint of the riches within.*

columns at its centre; this was probably never carried through because the Civil War intervened. De Caus's original plan of this projected design, which still survives, was improved, perhaps by Jones, with the addition of towers at each end.

### DOUBLE CUBE ROOM
While the building's facade has a classical, Italianate appearance, its extraordinary interior exhibits the influence of French style. The most celebrated of Jones's staterooms is the lavishly decorated Double Cube Room. This is not, in fact, the original room built in the 1630s, since a fire in 1647 or 1648 severely damaged the central part of the wing and the room was rebuilt and redecorated c.1648–53 by John Webb, under the direction of Jones, who was

### A COLLEGE OF THE 'LEARNED AND INGENIOUS'
Wilton House was the scene of great events in the Elizabethan and Jacobean periods, when Mary, Countess of Pembroke (wife of Henry Herbert, 2nd Earl of Pembroke) was a great literary hostess. The writer John Aubrey declared: 'In her time, Wilton House was like a college, there were so many learned and ingenious persons'. Mary was herself a poet and her brother was Sir Philip Sidney, who often stayed with her and wrote the bulk of his prose romance *The Arcadia* there before 1581. Christopher Marlowe, Edmund Spenser, Ben Jonson and John Donne certainly visited Wilton; some writers believe Shakespeare himself was a guest of the Countess of Pembroke and that *As You Like It* had its first performance at Wilton House on 2 December 1603, with James I in the audience.

then over 70 years old. The room is called Double Cube because of its dimensions: 60ft (18m) long by 30ft (9m) wide and 30ft (9m) high. It is decorated with expanses of fruit and flowers carved in wood and then gilded and fixed to the white walls. The chimney-pieces are of intricately carved Italian marble; the coved ceilings are equally ornate. On the walls hang portraits by Sir Anthony van Dyck of the Herberts and the royal family. The room is today furnished with lavish gilt mirrors, and red velvet chairs and sofas designed in the 18th century by William Kent and Thomas Chippendale. Beside it is the similarly lavishly decorated Single Cube Room, a perfect 30ft (9m) cube. The latest thinking is that the fire did not reach this room, and therefore it appears today as it was decorated in the 1630s. The lower panels on its walls retell the story of Philip Sidney's *The Arcadia*. In World War II, remarkably, the Double Cube Room was a military operations centre in which the D-Day landings were planned.

*Below: Wilton's Palladian bridge was the original of the three country-house bridges in this style. It was copied at Stowe (1738) and Prior Park, Bath (1756).*

## PALLADIAN BRIDGE

Wilton House is also celebrated for its Palladian-style bridge across the River Nadder, which flows through the grounds, built in 1737 by Henry Herbert, the 9th Earl of Pembroke. With its temple portico, it is one of three almost identical bridges of this period; others are to be found at Prior Park, Bath, and Stowe, Buckingham.

*Above: The Double Cube Room. Credit for its decorative scheme should go to Jean Barbet and John Webb – especially Webb, who redecorated it after the 1647–8 fire.*

In the 9th Earl's time, also, the gardens were landscaped in the 'picturesque style'; then, in 1779, Lancelot 'Capability' Brown was brought in to redesign them. At the start of the 19th century, Wyatt opened up the interior of the house by adding Gothic cloisters and building a new entrance via the north forecourt.

## WILTON'S POPULARITY

Wilton House was a great favourite of James I, and across the centuries it remained close to the heart of national life, visited frequently by the reigning monarch. It so impressed Daniel Defoe that he wrote 'One cannot be said to have seen anything that a man of curiosity would think worth seeing in the country and not have been at Wilton House'.

More recently, the house and grounds have become a star of the screen. Major productions filmed at Wilton have included *The Madness of King George*, *Mrs Brown*, *Sense and Sensibility* and the 2005 version of *Pride and Prejudice*.

# 'PLANTATION CASTLES' IN ULSTER
## BALFOUR, ENNISKILLEN, MONEA, TULLY AND KILLYLEAGH

In 1618, Scottish Protestant lord, Sir James Balfour, built Castle Balfour at Linaskea in County Fermanagh on the site of a fortress belonging to the Maguires, the leading family of Fermanagh since 1300. Sir James got the Maguire land as a beneficiary of James I's 'Plantation' of Ulster — the introduction of Protestant Englishmen and Scots into this rebellious and strongly Catholic part of northern Ireland.

Castle Balfour, now ruined, was built in the style of contemporary Scottish strong-houses, on a T-plan with stair turrets and parapets.

Another Maguire stronghold was rebuilt at nearby Enniskillen, County Fermanagh, by Captain William Cole – like Balfour, originally a man of Fife – in 1611. While living in a makeshift timber house, Cole reworked the ruined medieval fortress, adding a strong defensive wall and raising a new dwelling. He built a distinctively Scottish watergate to guard the entrance from the adjacent Lough Erne. It has twin turrets with conical roofs. Stylistic similarities

suggest that Enniskillen and Balfour castles may have been rebuilt by the same Scottish masons.

### SCOTTISH PROFILE AT MONEA
Castle Balfour and Enniskillen Castle are just two of several fortifications in Northern Ireland built or refashioned by Scottish or English incomers, who

*Above: Enniskillen's substantial twin-turreted gate was built to guard against a waterborne attack across Lough Erne.*

received their lands as part of the Plantation of Ulster. Near Enniskillen, the substantial Monea Castle was built c.1616 by Scottish churchman, Malcolm Hamilton, later Archbishop of Cashel. The rectangular three-storey stronghold, now ruined, was 50ft (15m) tall and 20ft (6m) wide, enclosed by a 300ft (91m) defensive circuit wall 9ft (2.7m) in height. On its west front stood two cylindrical towers with square rooms projecting diagonally at attic level – a distinctive profile probably copied from that of Claypotts Castle near Dundee in Scotland. The castle had a single entrance in the most northerly of these towers, with a spiral staircase leading to the well-lit main reception rooms, with big windows and window-seats, on the first floor and then to the bedrooms on the second floor.

Later, the castle was the residence of Gustavus Hamilton, Governor of Enniskillen and 1st Viscount Boyne. Hamilton was financially ruined during the Williamite Wars, during which he

---

### DUNLUCE: A MANSION WITHIN A CASTLE

In c.1620, Randal McDonnell, 1st Earl of Antrim, constructed an elegant manor house with gables and large mullioned windows within the fortifications of a 13th-century castle at Dunluce, County Antrim, on a basalt rock above the sea. He was the son of Scottish adventurer, Sorley Boy McDonnell, who captured the castle in c.1560 from members of the locally powerful McQuillan clan and, after being evicted, retook it from an English garrison. In 1586, Sorley Boy was made Constable of the Castle by Elizabeth I, but his loyalty was not beyond question – two years later, he reputedly gave refuge to survivors from a Spanish Armada

galleon, which had foundered on Atlantic rocks below the castle; he also armed his castle with cannon taken from the ship.

Randal McDonnell married Lady Katharine Manners, the widow of great court favourite the Earl of Buckingham, and brought her to live at Dunluce. They equipped their mansion lavishly – with the finest tapestries and, it is said, a pair of curtains from Hampton Court Palace. Its remains can be seen today within the castle walls, alongside the columns of an extraordinary sandstone loggia that Sorley Boy erected, along the lines of one built by the Earl of Bothwell at Crichton Castle near Edinburgh.

*Above: At Killyleagh, the original 17th-century towers are rather lost amid the mid-19th-century Scots Baronial reworking.*

was Brigadier General of William III's army. After his death in 1691, his family remained in residence at Monea for some time, but eventually were forced by money difficulties to sell the castle.

## TULLY CASTLE

Another Scottish planter, Sir John Hume of Berwick, built Tully Castle near Blaney village in County Fermanagh, overlooking Lower Lough Erne, in 1612-15. The village and area took the name Blaney from that of Sir Edward Blaney, who, as Lord Deputy in the service of King James I, had been despatched to Fermanagh to oversee and arrange the Plantation.

Tully Castle consisted of a defended enclosure or bawn, with four projecting rectangular corner towers, plus a two-and-half-storey fortified building. Today it is a substantial and picturesque ruin because it was captured and burned by Rory, scion of the Maguire family, during an attack on Christmas Day 1641 that was part of the bloody rebellion of that year by Irish Catholics. In the attack on Tully Castle, 16 men and 69 women and children were killed, although the Hume family survived.

## ROUGHAN CASTLE

Near Newmills in County Tyrone, Andrew Stewart built Roughan Castle in *c*.1618. His father was another Scottish nobleman and benificiary of the Plantation, Lord Castlestewart, who had founded Stewartstown, near Newmills. The three-storey castle has a 20ft (6m) central tower and four round corner towers. In the rebellion of 1641, the castle was held by Andrew Stewart's descendant Robert Stewart, who, after marrying into the O'Neill family, took the side of the rebels.

## KILLYLEAGH CASTLE

Another beneficiary of the Plantation was Sir James Hamilton of Ayrshire, who was granted large territories in County Down that had previously belonged to the O'Neill clan. He built Killyleagh Castle, with a round tower and conical roof, on the site of a 12th-century fortification raised by Norman adventurer-knight John de Courcy. The round tower survives on the south corner of the castle front; it is balanced by an identical tower on the north end of the front, added in the late 17th century following damage in the civil war. The castle was reworked in the Scottish Baronial style in the mid-19th century by Archibald Hamilton.

*Above: The ruins of Monea Castle give a good indication of its former grandeur – and show off the distinctive design of the tower.*

*Right: Monea Castle in its prime, c.1620. This view shows its distinctive round towers with square rooms projecting at attic level.*

# CHAPTER FOUR

# RESTORATION STYLE

### *c.1660–c.1714*

During the years of the Commonwealth and Protectorate, many of England's leading Royalists were forced to abandon their country houses to live in exile in Europe. During these years, they were impressed by French, Italian and Dutch styles of architecture, decoration and garden design. When they returned with Charles II at the Restoration of the Monarchy in 1660, many brought with them continental tastes for elaborate decoration.

Craftsmen such as the French metalworker Jean Tijou, the Dutch-born woodcarver Grinling Gibbons, and the Danish sculptor Caius Gabriel Cibber, worked on magnificent interiors for discerning patrons at houses such as Chatsworth, Petworth and Belton, for Charles II in his superb staterooms at Windsor Castle and, after the 'Glorious Revolution' of 1688, for William III and Mary II at Hampton Court Palace. Their work adorned Great Apartments – suites of grand reception rooms, which, in the 17th century, replaced the Great Hall as the principal feature of the great house and palace. These staterooms attempted to mirror the splendour of the chateaux and palaces of continental Europe, especially that of Louis XIV at Versailles. European taste and, in particular, Louis's great palace complex – a resounding expression of his absolute rule – also had an influence on the laying out of pleasure grounds around country houses and palaces in these years. At Hampton Court Palace, for example, both Charles II and, later, William and Mary created elaborate water and floral decorations in the French style.

*Left: The originally Tudor Chatsworth House, completely rebuilt in grand style by the 4th Earl of Devonshire in 1687–1707, stands in a beautiful position beside the River Derwent.*

# PETWORTH HOUSE
## AND GRINLING GIBBONS

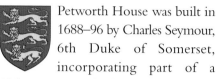

Petworth House was built in 1688–96 by Charles Seymour, 6th Duke of Somerset, incorporating part of a 13th-century castle that belonged to the Percy earls of Northumberland. The Duke's great house, which stands on the edge of the West Sussex town of Petworth, is renowned particularly for its association with artists and contains a room of woodcarving generally agreed to be the masterpiece of the great craftsman Grinling Gibbons.

Petworth House is often cited as a rare example of direct French influence on the English great house. Horace Walpole declared it to be 'in the style of the Tuileries', the royal palace that once stood alongside the Louvre in central Paris. Petworth's original west entrance front is thought to have featured a

### MASTER OF WOODCARVING: GRINLING GIBBONS

Born in Rotterdam, in 1648, to an English father, Gibbons had made his name in London as a wood carver by the early 1670s. He produced woodcarvings for Charles II at Windsor Castle and, in the 1680s–90s, made the carvings for Petworth House while also completing work at Hampton Court Palace and Kensington Palace, as commissioned by William III and Mary II. He was appointed Master Carver at the Royal Court in 1693. He also did exquisite work at St Paul's Cathedral, carving choir stalls and a fine organ screen, as well as working in stone on the exterior of Sir Christopher Wren's building (completed in 1710) and making a bronze statue of James II, now outside the National Gallery, London.

*Above: Gibbons' delicate work had an enduring influence on country house decor.*

*Below: Grinling Gibbons' carving on the picture frames at Petworth House is marked by a breathtaking realism and delicacy.*

central dome, with a series of elaborate urns around its cupola, while statues were arranged on the balustrade running across the entire front. This arrangement can be seen in a picture of the house *c.*1700, now at Belvoir Castle. However, the central dome was destroyed and the west front damaged in a fire of 1714. During restoration, the house was given a plainer appearance.

Even so, nine of the west front's 42 tall windows (three in the centre and three at each end) have busts and carving above them in a French style. The famous deer park at Petworth was landscaped by 'Capability' Brown in the 1750s.

### ENTRANCE HALL

Within, the house contains nine interconnecting staterooms arranged along the front, facing the park, and behind them nine equally grand rooms along the east, or town, side of the house. In the centre of the west front is the Marble Hall, originally the entrance hall,

with a floor of white, green and black marble, a fireplace at its north and south ends and elaborate carving by John Selden around the doors and fireplaces and above the cornice. (Selden worked on the estate for the Duke, yet, despite the superb quality of his work, is little known aside from Petworth House.) In the 19th century, the entrance was moved from the park side to the house's other main front, on the east side facing the town.

### GRINLING GIBBONS ROOM

Further along the front to the north is the Grinling Gibbons Room. In this large space, 20ft (6m) high, 24ft (7m) wide and 60ft (18m) long, Gibbons provided fantastically carved frames for seven portraits – including a large central one of Henry VIII, copied from the celebrated original of Hans Holbein. Gibbons' limewood-carving of flowers, fruit, leaves, musical instruments, birds, baskets and other intricate objects is wonderfully detailed and delicate.

### CHAPEL

The chapel at Petworth House is a survivor from the 13th-century castle of the Percy earls. To this, in 1690–2, the 6th Duke added a plaster ceiling together with stalls, altar rail and gallery in gilded wood.

### CAPTURED ON CANVAS

In the 1750s, Alicia Maria, Countess of Egremont, lavishly redecorated the sitting room now known as the White and Gold Room. This is probably the room painted by J.M.W. Turner in his celebrated picture *Drawing Room at Petworth*, now held by the National Gallery, London. This is one of a famous series of paintings by Turner, who visited several times in the 1830s as a friend of the 3rd Earl of Egremont.

### FRENCH INFLUENCE AT BOUGHTON

At the same time that Petworth House was being built, the main north front at Boughton House, Northamptonshire, was constructed in a French style by the francophile Ralph, 3rd Lord Montagu, who had served as Charles II's ambassador to France in 1669, 1676 and 1677. The front has a protruding

*Right: Gibbons' work in situ. Horace Walpole said the Gibbons Room at Petworth was 'the most superb monument of his skill'.*

pavilion at each end and between these a ground-floor loggia (arcade) that Montagu called 'the cloisters'. Above the arcade was the five-room Great Apartment floored with parquet in the style of Versailles.

Lord Montagu was a colourful and notable character: Jonathan Swift declared him to be 'as arrant a knave as any in his time', while William Congreve dedicated his play *The Way of the World* to him in 1700. Lord Montagu received

*Above: A regal French style in Sussex. The great west front at Petworth House faces the park and contains nine grand state rooms.*

William III in the splendid surroundings of Boughton House in 1695. He also built a fine town house, Montagu House, in London, which subsequently became the first home of the British Museum. In 1705, Queen Anne made Lord Montagu Marquess of Monthermer and 1st Duke of Montagu.

# HOLYROODHOUSE PALACE
## SCOTTISH ROYAL RESIDENCE

In the 1530s, James V raised a conical-turreted rectangular tower at Holyroodhouse in Edinburgh containing royal apartments (see page 28). The palace served as the principal residence of Mary, Queen of Scots, and witnessed the murder of her secretary, David Rizzio, at the hands of men led by Mary's husband, Lord Darnley. In the reign of Mary's son, James VI of Scots and I of England, the palace fell into decline but was renovated in time for the Scottish coronation of James's son and successor, Charles I. During the Civil War, Parliamentarian forces were housed in the palace, which was badly damaged by fire.

### CHARLES II'S RECONSTRUCTION WORK

During the 1670s, Charles II initiated a major reconstruction of the Palace of Holyroodhouse. Directed by Sir William Bruce, who was appointed Surveyor-General and Overseer of the King's

*Below: Charles II's rebuilding at Holyroodhouse transformed the building into an elegant palace in the classical style.*

Buildings in Scotland, and implemented by Robert Mylne, the King's Master Mason in Scotland, Charles's programme involved raising a southern tower on the entrance front to match the splendid northern one built by James V, and erecting a range between the towers with a fine Doric portico at the entrance. Fine classical façades were added to the inner quadrangle, with an elegant arcade at ground level.

The first floor contained the royal apartments, fitted with impressive plaster ceilings – especially in the West Drawing Room – and elegant wainscoting. In the Long Gallery, the Dutch artist Jacob de Wet painted 110 portraits of Scottish kings, both real and legendary, from Fergus I to Charles II, who commissioned the work. Charles also made the Holyrood Abbey Church the Chapel Royal for the palace. Charles, however, saw none of this fine work, as he did not once visit Holyroodhouse.

### LATER DEVELOPMENTS

During the brief reign of Charles's successor, the Roman Catholic James VII of Scots and II of England, the King

*Above: Charles II and James, Duke of York. James was deposed before he could enjoy the alterations he made at Holyroodhouse.*

adapted the chapel so it could be used for Roman Catholic rites. In later years, his grandson 'Bonnie Prince Charlie' stayed at Holyroodhouse Palace for a few weeks in 1745, during his attempt to win the throne back for his father, but after the collapse of the '45 revolt no royal stayed there until Queen Victoria in the 19th century. Renovated in Victorian times and by George V, the Palace has regained its position as Scotland's foremost royal palace. It is Queen Elizabeth II's official residence when she visits Scotland each year.

# WINDSOR CASTLE
## AND CHARLES II

Windsor Castle was Charles II's favourite royal residence outside London, and he undertook a major rebuilding scheme there in the 1670s. Using Hugh May as architect, Antonio Verrio as principal artist and Grinling Gibbon for decorative carving, Charles built new state apartments and redecorated St George's Hall and the King's Chapel at an overall cost of £130,000. Much of this splendid work was remodelled in the 19th century by George IV and Sir Jeffry Wyatville, but elements of the 1670s' alterations survive in the King's Dining Room, in the Queen's Presence and Audience Chambers and (outside) in the Long Walk, lined with elms for its 3 mile (4.5km) route from the south entrance of the castle to Windsor Great Park.

### THE UPPER WARD

Externally, Hugh May rebuilt the castle's upper ward in a largely classical style. Its east front, for example, had four massive towers and a central *piano nobile* accessed by two staircases. Internally, the lavish state apartments attempted to replicate some of the magnificence of Versailles. They are identified by some architectural historians as the first English apartments in the Baroque style and were the inspiration for

*Below: Charles II laid out the imposing Long Walk, lined with elms, approaching Windsor Castle across the Great Park.*

sets of similarly magnificent staterooms at houses such as Burghley and Chatsworth. The king and queen had separate suites of apartments, including drawing rooms, audience chambers and bedchambers; the queen also had a ballroom. Gibbons' naturalistic carving of game birds, flowers, fruit and fish adorned the walls, which were also wainscoted; 13 ceiling paintings by Verrio represented the triumphs of the King and the Church of England.

### ST GEORGE'S HALL

Charles's redecorated St George's Hall also featured grand historical-allegorical paintings by Verrio, depicting scenes from the history of the Order of the Garter, together with Charles II enthroned in grandeur. The hall was fitted with a gilt throne made by John van der Stein and Louis von Opstal.

### GIBBONS' WORK IN EVIDENCE

Some of Gibbons' carving survives today in the Waterloo Chamber, which was created by George IV in the 1820s. In addition, the Royal Chapel contained wooden stalls carved in the shape of

*Above: This reconstruction shows St George's Hall in the 1670s – as decorated by Verrio and Gibbons for Charles II.*

laurel and palm by Gibbons; the walls were decorated with a set of Verrio murals depicting Christ's miracles, while the ceiling celebrated the Resurrection. Behind the altar was a version of the *Last Supper* and columns derived from Gian Lorenzo Bernini's Baroque-style *baldechino* (canopy) in St Peter's, Rome.

### AN UNFINISHED PALACE

Charles II began a grand new royal residence at Winchester to replace the medieval castle and palace there. Building was begun in 1682 to designs by Sir Christopher Wren that aimed to replicate the glory of Versailles on English soil. At Charles's death in 1685, the shell of the building was complete. But thereafter work was stopped by James II, and Wren's building was never fitted out internally. The 'palace' was later used as a military barracks before burning down in 1894.

# CHATSWORTH
## 'PALACE OF THE PEAK'

Chatsworth's superbly grand appearance, lavish interior, magnificent works of art and splendid gardens in a wonderful setting combine to make it one of the finest – and perhaps the most famous – of all England's stately homes. The house, which stands in the glorious countryside of the Derbyshire Peak District, is celebrated as 'the Palace of the Peak'.

The first major house at Chatsworth was built in the mid-16th century by Elizabeth Cavendish (later 'Bess of Hardwick', builder of Hardwick House) and her second husband, Sir William Cavendish, Treasurer of the Chamber at the court of King Henry VIII. This house was completely rebuilt in 1687–1707 by William Cavendish, the 4th Earl of Devonshire.

A long wing was built to the north of the 4th Earl's elegant house in the 19th century by yet another William Cavendish, 6th Duke of Devonshire, to the designs of architect Sir Jeffry Wyatville.

*Below: Baroque aesthetics? This riot of figures is a detail from one of Laguerre's exuberant ceilings at Chatsworth.*

*Above: Garden diversion. The cascade installed in 1696 created interesting sound effects, as well as being a visual delight.*

### REBUILDING CHATSWORTH

The 16th-century house stood on the same site as the one we see today, on a terrace beside the River Derwent, and like its successor it was built around a central courtyard. In 1687, the 4th Earl began with the intention of rebuilding only the south front of this house, but when he found that this improvement showed up imperfections in the other parts of the house, he was persuaded to move on to another part, and then another. He intended each improvement to be the last, but in the end, over the course of 20 years, he rebuilt Chatsworth entirely, one section at a time.

The new south and east wings were designed by William Talman, then an unknown architect. Talman grew increasingly frustrated by the Earl's autocratic behaviour, particularly his habit of changing his mind and tearing down

### JEAN TIJOU

The supremely skilled metalworker, Jean Tijou, was a French Huguenot who came to England as a religious exile after 1685. He did exquisite work at Hampton Court Palace and its gardens and made screens and grilles for St Paul's Cathedral, as well as working at Chatsworth, Burghley House, Castle Howard and Easton Neston. The 'Golden Gates' he provided at Chatsworth are matched by his intricate gilded iron gates at Burghley House.

## A KENNEDY AT CHATSWORTH

In 1944, William, Marquess of Hartington, eldest son of the 10th Duke of Devonshire and heir to Chatsworth House, married an American bride, Kathleen Kennedy, whose brother John F. Kennedy would in 1961 become the 35th President of the United States. William was killed in action that same year, and his young wife lived only four years as the Marchioness of Hartington before herself dying in an air accident in 1948. Her portrait is displayed in the Sketch Galleries at Chatsworth House; she is buried at the churchyard of St Peter in the village of Edensor on the Chatsworth estate – in the same graveyard as the 6th Duke of Devonshire and Joseph Paxton.

building work that had already been completed. The relationship was soured further by prolonged disputes over payment, which resulted in Sir Christopher Wren being despatched to Chatsworth in 1692 to make a judgement on how much the building had cost to that date: his arbitration was the sum of £9,025 16s 6¾d. As a result of this quarrel, Talman was not involved in the rebuilding of the west and north fronts. The west front was probably designed by Thomas Archer, while the north front may have been the work of the Earl himself (from 1694, the 1st Duke of Devonshire) or perhaps was created by John Fitch or even Wren.

### LAVISH INTERIORS

The interior of the new house was lavishly decorated and fitted out by the finest craftsmen. Louis Laguerre painted the chapel frescoes (which have remained unaltered since 1694) and, together with Antonio Verrio and Ricard, decorated the ceilings of the staterooms and staircase. These rooms are arranged on the top floor of the three-storey house and provide marvellous views of the park outside. The great stone staircase has a fine wrought-iron balustrade by Frenchman Jean Tijou; a second staircase rises beneath a coved ceiling by Sir James Thornhill, who also painted the illusionist decoration in the Sabine Room. In the State Music Room, the Dutch artist, Jan van der Vaart, painted another widely celebrated *trompe l'oeil*: an image of a very realistic violin hanging on a door.

### THE GARDENS AND PARK

The extensive gardens and parkland we see today were largely created in the 18th century by 'Capability' Brown and in the 19th century by the 6th Duke, his architect Sir Jeffry Wyatville, and his gardener Joseph Paxton (later designer of the Crystal Palace in London). However, the Great Cascade, the stepped waterfall that descends the slope behind the house, was designed in the 1st Duke's time by Thomas Archer in 1696. Waters from the moorland above feed into a 'Cascade House' and then run down the slope for around ¼ mile (0.4km) over steps varying in size and shape, which alter the sound made by the water as it falls. When the Great Cascade was built, Chatsworth's grounds contained formal terraces and parterres designed by the foremost landscape gardeners of their day: George London and Henry Wise.

*Below: Chatsworth probably looks at its most beautiful when the rich hues of its stonework are set off by autumnal leaves.*

# FELBRIGG HALL
## AN ARCHITECTURAL CURIOSITY

In the L-shaped country house of Felbrigg Hall, near Cromer in Norfolk, a Jacobean wing of 1621–4 meets at right angles with a classical wing of *c.*1680. Two architectural languages, the first native English, the second classical in origin, though only 60 years apart, meet here in curious juxtaposition.

### LYMINGE'S JACOBEAN WING

The first Felbrigg Hall was medieval. Thomas Windham demolished all except the cellars when he commissioned Robert Lyminge to build a new house.

Lyminge's Jacobean wing has seven bays, including the central porch, and a homely rustic appearance, being built of a combination of flint, brick and stone. Within, the house originally contained a hall and kitchen on the ground floor, a bedchamber and private saloon on the second floor and a Long Gallery along the length of the third floor. Although these

*Above: Two houses in one at Felbrigg. This view shows the Jacobean wing, with the classical wing just visible facing to the left.*

rooms have been restructured in the intervening years, the actual façade remains largely untouched.

### ENGLAND'S FIRST CLASSICAL PORTICO

The Vyne in Hampshire, built by Tudor courtier Lord Sandys, was owned during the Commonwealth period by Chaloner Chute, the Speaker of the House of Commons. In *c.*1654, he commissioned John Webb to build a classical portico on the house's north front, which was the first structure of its kind in the country.

*Below: The first classical portico in an English country house looks out across the lake in the grounds of The Vyne.*

### SAMWELL'S CLASSICAL WING

In 1675–86, Thomas Windham's son, William, built a contrasting classical wing, which was designed by gentleman architect William Samwell, with fine red brickwork, 16 tall windows and six small dormers in the roof. It connects with the Jacobean wing at the corner, but the two wings make no concessions to each other.

### PAINE'S REMODELLED ROOMS

In 1749–56, William Windham's grandson, William Windham II, commissioned the architect James Paine to remodel the three main rooms on the ground floor of the 1680s wing. One, originally the entrance hall, he made the Dining Room; a second was the Drawing Room; the third, called 'the Cabinet', he fitted with red damask on the walls as a backing for a collection of paintings brought back by his patron from a continental Grand Tour.

In an upstairs room, Paine created a fine Gothic library to house William Windham II's large book collection. It is considered a splendid example of the early Gothic Revival style.

# NOTTINGHAM CASTLE
## A DUCAL MANSION

William the Conqueror first established a timber fortress in Nottingham in the year after the Conquest. In 1170, Henry III built a stone castle on the same elevated site, establishing Nottingham Castle as the most important and formidable royal castle in the Midlands. Finally, William Cavendish, 1st Duke of Newcastle, and his son Henry, 2nd Duke, erected a ducal mansion on this historic site in 1674–9.

The castle witnessed numerous important events in the medieval period. In 1194, King Richard I the Lionheart used siege machinery to take the castle from his brother John (the future King John), who had seized power while Richard was on Crusade. Then, in 1330, Edward III broke into the castle through a 300ft (91m)-long subterranean passageway, surprising his mother, Queen Isabella, and her lover, Roger Mortimer, Earl of March, who together were the effective rulers of the country, although Edward wore the crown. Mortimer was executed in London. The passageway, known as Mortimer's Hole, can be seen in the

*Below: Nottingham Castle – a ducal mansion rather than a fortress. Its elevated position gives it superb views of the city.*

*Right: An artwork reconstruction shows clearly the size of the original Nottingham Castle – and its imposing situation.*

grounds. In 1485, Richard III rode out from Nottingham Castle to Bosworth Field, the battlefield on which he lost his crown to Henry Tudor, the future Henry VII and father of Henry VIII.

### IN AND OUT OF ROYAL HANDS
In 1623, James I granted the castle and its adjacent parkland to Francis Manners, 6th Earl of Rutland. In the Civil War, Nottingham Castle was a rallying point for King Charles I, who raised the royal standard there in 1642. It was later garrisoned for Parliament under the command of Colonel John Hutchinson. His troops repulsed several royalist attempts to capture the castle. Then, after Charles I's execution in 1649, the stronghold was demolished on the orders of Parliament.

### 'PROSPECT HOUSE'
The mansion the 1st and 2nd Dukes built on the site of the original castle, was a 'prospect house': perched on its high rock, it had superb views over the town and parkland. The house had two wings. The staterooms for grand receptions were on the first floor. In the early

Hanoverian years, Thomas Pelham, the then Duke of Newcastle, was twice prime minister (1754–6 and 1757–62).

In the 19th century, the mansion was severely damaged when, in 1831, rioters protesting in favour of parliamentary reform broke into the house and started a great fire. (Its owner, Henry, 4th Duke of Newcastle, was a well-known opponent of reform.) The conflagration reduced the building to a shell, but it was restored and refurbished as an art gallery in 1878.

# BELTON HOUSE
## 'A GLORIOUS HOUSE'

The elegant Belton House, near Grantham, was built in 1685–8 for Sir John Brownlow, High Sheriff of Lincolnshire. It is ranked as one of England's finest examples of a late 17th-century country house.

We know disappointingly little about Sir John Brownlow himself. He wed his cousin and fathered five lively daughters, and apart from being High Sheriff of Lincolnshire, he was twice MP for Grantham. Belton House was sufficiently grand for Sir John to entertain William III there in 1695, but two years later he took his own life.

### CHRISTOPHER WREN AS ROYAL ARCHITECT

Sir Christopher Wren is celebrated above all for his design of the rebuilt St Paul's Cathedral (and 52 other London churches). Yet he was also a significant royal architect, serving as the monarch's Surveyor of Works from 1669 to 1718, for Charles II, James II, William III and Mary II, Anne and George I. Wren was influenced not only by the classical architecture of Inigo Jones and John Webb in England, but also by the magnificent Louvre and Versailles palaces, which he saw on a trip to France in the 1660s. He was Professor of Astronomy at Oxford University and a founder and President of the Royal Society (an elite scientific body in London), and thus brought a vast intellect and a fresh outlook to his architectural work. He provided designs for rebuilding Whitehall Palace, designed a new palace (never finished) for Charles II at Winchester, made alterations to the Queen's Chapel, St James's, and added a small block of new staterooms there. Wren also designed the Royal Naval Hospital in Greenwich, in addition to substantial work at Hampton Court Palace and Kensington Palace. His range was wide: some claim him as an architect of the monumental Baroque (there are certainly elements of this style in some of his church designs), while others prefer to emphasize his more conventional work, which was carried out in a classical Renaissance style.

*Left: Sir Christopher Wren, associated forever with the dome of St Paul's Cathedral, may have designed Belton House.*

*Above: The south (right) and west fronts at Belton House. Note James Wyatt's elegant neoclassical doorway of 1777.*

His architect is not known, although possible names mentioned by historians are William Winde, William Stanton and even Sir Christopher Wren. The design was closely based on that of Clarendon House on Piccadilly, London. This building, designed by Sir Roger Pratt for Edward Hyde, Earl of Clarendon, was highly regarded by contemporaries (Pepys called it 'the finest pile I ever saw in my life … a glorious house'), but it was demolished in 1683 after the Earl's fall from favour and flight to France.

### MELLOW STONE EXTERIOR

The H-shaped house at Belton has two near-identical façades: to the south is the main entrance and to the north the garden front. Thirteen large windows arrayed in two symmetrical lines of seven fill the main section of the front, between protruding end wings that are each two bays wide.

The north front has been unchanged since building, but on the entrance front James Wyatt added a neoclassical doorway with pilasters (flattened columns) and entablature (decorative carving above the columns) in 1777. The house is built of ashlar dressed stone from the quarry at nearby Ancaster, which has weathered delightfully over the years to give the house a mellow look.

### INTERIOR GRANDEUR

The interior is lavishly decorated with woodcarving and stucco work. The Marble Hall and Saloon have exquisite limewood carving by the great Grinling Gibbons; the chapel has a wonderfully carved original reredos (ornamental screen) that may also be by Gibbons. The chapel is virtually unaltered and it and the Chapel Gallery also contain fine plaster ceilings modelled by Edward Goudge. The wall panelling in the Chapel Drawing Room is delicately painted to simulate marble.

### ALTERATION AND RESTORATION

Upstairs, the Tyrconnel Room is a rare example of a late 18th-century painted floor: it features the arms of the Brownlow family amid decorative foliage. In *c.*1776–7, James Wyatt built the splendid library, which has a barrel-vaulted ceiling.

In the early 19th century, Sir Jeffry Wyatville added a fine staircase to Belton House and created the elegant

---

### THE 'LADY ARCHITECT' OF WESTON PARK

Elizabeth, Lady Wilbrahim, rebuilt Weston Park in Shropshire in the 1670s. She designed in the classical idiom – visitors can see her copy of Palladio's *First Book of Architecture* annotated with notes for redesigning the house. But her house also exhibits French influence, in its semicircular pediments, and Dutch style in its combination of brick and stone. She inherited the medieval house that stood on the site, and then acquired wealth through marriage to Sir Thomas Wilbrahim in 1651. This remarkable woman also designed the parish church and stables at Weston Park.

Weston Park contains a magnificent art collection, including works by Holbein and van Dyck. It stands in an estate of 1000 acres (404ha), in parkland landscaped by 'Capability' Brown in 1765; in the 1770s, James Paine built a Temple of Diana in the grounds.

*Above: Weston Park was designed by Elizabeth, Lady Wilbrahim, in the 1670s in the Palladian style.*

In the 19th century, it was often visited by Prime Minister Benjamin Disraeli, who had an intense platonic relationship with Selina, Countess of Bradford, wife of the house's then owner, the 3rd Earl of Bradford. A collection of 1,100 letters from Disraeli to the Countess is displayed at the house. In modern times, the house was the venue for the G8 summit of world leaders in 1998.

---

Red Drawing Room, which has a wonderful *trompe l'oeil* frieze together with panels of crimson damask set in the wainscoting. The room is hung with a wealth of pictures, including a number of works by Van Dyck, Titian and Rembrandt.

Outside, Wyatville built an orangery and fountain and laid out an Italian garden. Later in the 19th century, the 3rd Earl of Brownlow sensitively restored Belton House, in particular rebuilding the balustrade and cupola on the roof.

### ROYAL CONNECTIONS

Belton House sits in 36 acres (14ha) of fine formal and semi-formal gardens and a large landscaped park. The house remained in the hands of Sir John Brownlow's descendants until 1984, when it passed to the care of the National Trust. George III visited, as did Edward VIII before his abdication, at a time when the then Lord Brownlow was Lord-in-Waiting to the King. The library at Belton contains a display of objects associated with Edward VIII.

*Left: Belton's 19th-century orangery, Italianate fountain and garden were designed by Sir Jeffry Wyatville.*

# HAMPTON COURT, KENSINGTON PALACE
## AND THE WORK OF SIR CHRISTOPHER WREN

In 1689, William III and Mary II commissioned Sir Christopher Wren to rebuild Hampton Court Palace. Wren's intention was to sweep away the Tudor palace (see pages 20–1), retaining only the Great Hall, and to create a majestic Renaissance-style country residence grand enough to rival Louis XIV's palace at Versailles. In the event, due to lack of money and time (William and Mary were impatient to see results), Wren built only new sets of apartments for the King and Queen.

### THE FOUNTAIN COURT

The apartments were around a new courtyard, the Fountain Court, which Wren raised on the site of the former royal lodgings. The building work also created a new east front for the palace. The King and Queen, who ruled as joint monarchs, were to have separate sets of rooms accessed by separate grand staircases.

*Below: In red brick with Portland stone dressing, the east front at Hampton Court is a handsome example of Anglo-Dutch style.*

*Above: Detail of Wren's windows in the new east front at Hampton Court.*

Work began in 1689 and was completed by 1694. The new buildings featured the finest stone carving by Grinling Gibbons and Caius Gabriel Cibber, as well as splendid ironwork by Jean Tijou. However, following Mary's death that year, William halted the work before the interiors were decorated. In 1698, after the destruction of Whitehall Palace in a vast fire, William

*Above: William's and Mary's initials are intertwined on a Hampton Court façade.*

ordered the resumption of work at Hampton Court. The interior decoration, under the supervision of William Talman and with the King's personal involvement, continued until 1702. The ceilings above the staircase and in the King's staterooms were painted by Antonio Verrio.

### HAMPTON COURT GARDENS

Charles II had laid out a long 'canal' or elongated pond before the east front of the palace in 1668. William III filled in part of the 'canal' to create a parterre (a display of ornamental flowerbeds), designed by the Huguenot Daniel Marot. Working with the garden designer George London and with William Talman as architect, William also laid out a Privy Garden in the area between the palace and the River Thames and the Bushy Park Avenue to the north of the palace. The gardens contained splendid ironwork gates by Jean Tijou and architectural ornament by Cibber and Edward Pearce.

The Privy Garden was meticulously restored in 1991–5 with great concern for historical accuracy.

## THE MOVE TO KENSINGTON

Asthma-sufferer William III was advised by his doctors to move away from the smog-polluted atmosphere produced by countless coal fires around Whitehall Palace. He found it easier to breathe the country air at Hampton Court, but in winter he suffered even there on account of the mists rising from the Thames. His search for a conveniently situated winter residence ended at Kensington, then well outside London.

## THE NEW PALACE

William bought Nottingham House, a relatively modest Jacobean mansion built in about 1605 and owned by Daniel Finch, 2nd Earl of Nottingham, for around £20,000. Sir Christopher Wren enlarged it by adding a pavilion on each corner; he also moved the entrance to the west front, where he raised a two-storey portico and an entrance courtyard accessed through a clock-tower gateway.

The rebuilding began in July 1689 and was carried out very quickly, for William and Mary were in a great hurry to move in. In their haste, strict supervision of the site must have been lacking, for during that November part of the King's staterooms collapsed, killing eight labourers.

### KENSINGTON GARDENS

Some 26 acres (10.5ha) of formal gardens at Kensington Palace were created by Queen Mary and Henry Wise. During Anne's reign, a big Baroque orangery was built by Sir John Vanbrugh. In about 1730, the Round Pond was created in Kensington Palace Gardens for Caroline, wife of George II, and the gardens were opened to the public *c.* 1830.

*Left: The Great Staircase at Kensington Palace was later painted by William Kent.*

*Right: No flourishes. John Evelyn thought Kensington Palace 'a very sweet villa'.*

*Above: Marot's formal east front gardens, which replaced Charles II's canal, remain one of the glories of Hampton Court.*

# EASTON NESTON
## AND NICHOLAS HAWKSMOOR

Designed by Nicholas Hawksmoor, star pupil of Sir Christopher Wren, in 1696–1702, Easton Neston is often seen as a forerunner of the English Baroque style.

The patron, Sir William Fermor, 1st Lord Leominster, originally offered the job to Sir Christopher Wren, to whom he was related by marriage, around 1680. Then, or shortly afterwards, Sir Christopher designed two wings for the house, which were built, but the main house itself was not designed or constructed – probably because money was short. However, in 1692, after Fermor had made an advantageous marriage, he turned again to the project, and Wren recommended Hawksmoor, who designed and constructed Easton Neston unsupervised. Because the other

major houses he was involved with (Castle Howard and Blenheim Palace) were undertaken in collaboration with Vanbrugh, Easton Neston is remembered as the only country house that this remarkable architect built alone.

### PILASTERS AND COLUMNS

Hawksmoor's house is a small-scale palace. Built from the finest cream-coloured Helmdon stone (also used at Blenheim Palace and Stowe), Easton Neston is rectangular, with three storeys on the two main façades: first a ground floor, then two equal upper storeys each containing eight tall windows. At the four corners and between all the windows, pilasters (decorative features of attached pillars or columns) rise the entire height of the façade. On the entrance front, two rounded Corinthian columns, one

*Above: In 1876, this engraving of Easton Neston and part of the grounds was printed in the* Illustrated London News.

on either side of the door, rise to a round-topped pediment cut with the Fermor arms and motto *Hora e sempre* ('Now and forever'). Above the door, in line with the top-storey windows, is an arched 'Venetian window', while at roof level a balustrade is adorned with urns on top of each of the pilasters. The windows on the shorter sides of the house reveal the fact that it contains two 'mezzanine' floors for servants between the main floors of the house, making five storeys in all.

### GRANDIOSE PLANS

Hawksmoor drew plans for a large and elaborate forecourt at Easton Neston. He suggested building two side wings to house stables on one side and servants' rooms on the other, and a splendid colonnade flanking the entrance. He did build the entrance piers (which are still standing) and the stable block (quickly demolished), but otherwise these grandiose plans did not come to fruition.

### INTERIOR ALTERATIONS

The interior of Easton Neston has been changed somewhat since Hawksmoor built it – notably the Drawing Room was elaborately decorated with intricate

---

### NICHOLAS HAWKSMOOR

Like his mentor, Sir Christopher Wren, Nicholas Hawksmoor is remembered above all as a church architect. Hawksmoor worked with Wren on the rebuilding of St Paul's Cathedral, built several superb London churches and designed the

towers on the west front of Westminster Abbey. He also played a major role in building Castle Howard and Blenheim Palace, in addition to Easton Neston.

Born around 1660 in Nottinghamshire, Hawksmoor began working for Wren by 1680. His career advanced swiftly: before his 40th birthday, he was working alongside Vanbrugh at Castle Howard. For many years his work was overshadowed by that of Vanbrugh and Wren, but today he is increasingly seen as a highly original and gifted architect who combined the classicism of Wren with the Baroque of Vanbrugh. Hawksmoor also designed a new quadrangle at All Souls College, Oxford University, combining a classical interior with a Gothic exterior. He died in London in 1736.

*Left: The West Front at Westminster Abbey. The lower part was built in the 15th century, the towers added by Hawksmoor.*

---

*Above: Hawksmoor's design for Easton Neston exudes stately elegance. His grand plans for a dramatic Baroque-style use of space with a forecourt and side wings were, unfortunately, not brought to fruition.*

plasterwork in the mid-18th century and his large hall divided in two in the late 19th century to make a dining room alongside a smaller hall. However, the other main rooms remain unchanged, and on a bright day are flooded with light through the tall windows that rise almost from floor to ceiling, as does the elegant staircase with Tijou-style balustrade in wrought iron.

### CHANGE OF OWNERSHIP

Easton Neston remained in the hands of Sir William Fermor's descendants for a little over three centuries, always as a private home and never open to the public. But the costs of renovation following a fire in July 2002 severely

tested the family finances, and in 2005 Lord Hesketh sold the house and part of its 3,319-acre (1,343ha) estate to St Petersburg-born US-based fashion businessman, Leon Max.

### A BAROQUE BUILDING?

In contrast with other leading architects of his day, Hawksmoor made no voyages to see Italian and French buildings at first hand, and his classical influences all came via the study of reproductions in books. Architectural historians see elements at Easton Neston derived from the mid-16th-century palaces built by Michelangelo in the Piazza del Campidoglio on the Capitoline Hill in Rome. But, especially in Hawksmoor's large-scale courtyard design that was never built, continental influences prevail. There are also traces of the Baroque – the dramatic and exuberant monumental style more fully expressed in later houses, such as Castle Howard and

Blenheim Palace, on which Hawksmoor worked with Sir John Vanbrugh. Easton Neston can be seen as a forerunner of these buildings, an early flowering of the English Baroque. It also anticipates the Petit Trianon at Versailles, built in 1762–8 by Ange-Jacques Gabriel for Louis XV's mistress, Madame de Pompadour.

*Below: Easton Neston's owner in the 1930s, Thomas Fermor-Hesketh (1st Baron Hesketh), stands between his daughters.*

# MARLBOROUGH HOUSE
## AND THE CHURCHILLS

Marlborough House, alongside St James's Palace in Pall Mall, London, was built in 1709–11 to plans by Sir Christopher Wren for John Churchill, 1st Duke of Marlborough, and his wife, Sarah, Duchess of Marlborough and close friend of Queen Anne. The Duchess was the driving force behind the project, arranging a lease on the land, selecting Wren as architect – rather than Sir John Vanbrugh, who was then engaged by the Duke on Blenheim Palace – and, indeed, overseeing the final stages of building herself.

The dignified, originally two-storey house was, as the Duchess requested of Wren, 'strong, plain and convenient'. The design may have been drawn by Wren's son, also called Christopher, with his father's guidance. Its red bricks came from Holland, and had been carried as ballast in ships returning from taking supplies to the Duke of Marlborough's armies in the Low Countries.

The house contains the grand two-storey Saloon with paintings by Louis Laguerre of the Duke's triumph at the Battle of Blenheim. The ceiling features a painting by Orazio Gentileschi,

originally in the entrance hall of the Queen's House, Greenwich, but removed to Marlborough House at the start of the 18th century with Queen Anne's approval. The magnificent Ramillies Staircase, with black marble steps, ascends beneath paintings by Laguerre of scenes from another of the Duke's great battles, Ramillies.

The Duke of Marlborough died in 1722 and his body lay in state in Marlborough House prior to his funeral in Westminster Abbey. The Duchess died

*Above: 'Strong, plain and convenient' – and, with Hampton Court, another example of the Anglo-Dutch strain in Wren's output.*

after a long widowhood at Marlborough House in 1744. Sir William Chambers extended the house in the 1770s, increasing it from the original two to three storeys.

### A ROYAL PALACE

In 1817, the land and the house that stood on it reverted to the Crown. Marlborough House was the London residence of Edward, Prince of Wales (the future Edward VII), and his wife, Princess Alexandra of Denmark, from 1863 to 1901 and was immortalized in the popular name for the Prince's raffish friends, the 'Marlborough House set'. The future George V was born at Marlborough House, in 1865, and lived there while Prince of Wales in the 1900s.

Later, it was twice the home of widowed queens, first of Edward VII's widow, Alexandra, in 1910–25, and then of George V's widow, Mary, in 1936–53. In 1965, the house became home to the Commonwealth Secretariat and the Commonwealth Foundation and today is used for international conferences.

### JOHN CHURCHILL, 1ST DUKE OF MARLBOROUGH

The 1st Duke of Marlborough is renowned as one of England's greatest generals. His reputation rests on the series of great victories he won over the army of Louis XIV of France, most famously at Blenheim (1704), Ramillies (1706) and Oudenarde (1708); the Baroque masterpiece of Blenheim Palace in Oxfordshire was begun as a gift from Queen Anne and country in gratitude for the first of these. Before these years of greatness, he had survived disgrace, including imprisonment in 1691, when he was suspected of plotting to restore James II to the throne.

*Above: John Churchill by Christian Linke.*

# UPPARK
## AN ELEGANT COUNTRY HOUSE

The delightful country house of Uppark near Petersfield in West Sussex commands a breathtaking view of the South Downs. It was built *c.*1690 for Ford, Lord Grey of Werke, who was created Earl of Tankerville in 1695. Some authorities identify the architect as William Talman, who was dismissed around this time by Sir William Cavendish, 1st Duke of Devonshire, from Chatsworth House.

### AN ELEGANT DWELLING

Uppark was built on the site of an earlier house in a well-established country park belonging to the lords Grey. It has an elegant brick and stone south façade of nine bays, and the arms of a later owner, Sir Matthew Fetherstonhaugh, affixed to the pediment that rises over the central upper-floor windows. Of particular interest are the highly decorated modillions, or brackets, that support the roof cornice and the pediment.

Uppark is also celebrated for its elegant 18th-century interiors, installed by Sir Matthew and his wife, Sarah. The principal rooms include a Saloon that recalls in its lavish decoration the Double Cube Room at Wilton House.

### LADY HAMILTON

An Uppark resident of note in the late 18th century was Emma Hart, later better known as Lady Hamilton, wife of Sir William Hamilton and mistress of Horatio, Lord Nelson. In 1781, aged around 18, Emma lived at Uppark as the mistress of Sir Harry Fetherstonhaugh. The table in the dining room is the one on which Emma is said to have danced naked for Sir Harry and his friends.

*Above: The splendid brick and stone south front at Uppark, with the Featherstonhaugh arms in the pediment.*

### A PHOENIX FROM THE ASHES

Following a disastrous fire, which gutted the house in 1989, Uppark became a virtual laboratory for the latest techniques in meticulous architectural restoration. As part of this restoration by the National Trust, the gardens were remade in line with the 18th-century designs of Humphry Repton.

*Left: Gilded opulence. The lavish interiors of Uppark provided an arena for gracious living.*

### THE HOUSEKEEPER'S SON

The novelist H.G. Wells, author of *The Time Machine* and *The War of the Worlds*, spent some of his early years at Uppark, where his mother, Sarah Neal, was a ladies' maid and housekeeper in the 1870s–80s. At the time, Wells was trying to make his way in the world, and returned a number of times to Uppark after failed placements as a draper's apprentice, a chemist's assistant and a teacher. Wells wrote in his autobiography that 'the place had a great effect on me'; and he certainly took full advantage of Uppark's splendid library.

# GLOSSARY

**architrave** Part of the entablature (upper part) of a classical order. The architrave is the lintel (horizontal beam) directly above the top of the column and beneath the frieze. Also the moulded pane of a window or door.

**bailey** Area enclosed by the walls of a castle; also called 'ward'. Compare motte, the mound on which the keep was built. The most common early Norman castles consisted of a motte (with an, initially, wooden and, later, stone tower) and a bailey enclosed by an earthwork wall topped with a palisade.

**barbican** Heavily fortified defensive structure, often a double tower, usually built out from the castle gateway.

**Baronial** Style of Scottish architecture, employed only rarely in England, in vogue from the early 1800s until *c.*1920. The Baronial style used towers with small turrets, stepped gables and crenellations to create the appearance of a 'fairytale castle', such as Balmoral Castle.

**Baroque** Sensuous and dramatic style in art and architecture, originating in Rome around 1600, that found expression in highly ornamented, monumental buildings set in grand, landscaped parks. English Baroque buildings in *c.*1700–30 are characterized by their dramatic use of space and movement, surface ornamentation and dynamic interaction with their setting. Great examples include Castle Howard and Blenheim Palace.

**basilica** In ancient Roman buildings, a big public hall.

**bastide** Walled town built alongside a castle. Originally, a French term, but applied to castle-town developments, such as Conwy in Wales.

**bastion** Projecting fortification on the curtain wall of a castle.

**battlements** Low defensive wall or parapet on the top of a castle's curtain wall or its towers, with indented sections (*embrasures* or *crenelles*) and raised parts (*merlons* or *cops*). Battlements were later

*Above: Mullions and transoms on windows at Hampton Court Palace.*

used for decoration to give homes the appearance of a castle.

**bay** Section of a house's outer wall, defined by vertical features, such as windows, columns and pilasters.

**belvedere** Raised building or room that commands a fine view.

**burgh** Anglo-Saxon fortified town.

**chinoiserie** Originally, French term for interior decoration that mimicked Chinese arts and colour schemes. Starting in the 17th century, chinoiserie remained in vogue until the 19th century.

**classical** Style in English architecture pioneered by Inigo Jones in the 17th century, inspired by buildings of ancient Greece and Rome and Italian Renaissance interpretations of them. Fine examples of Jones's classical architecture in England include the Queen's House, Greenwich, and the Banqueting Hall, Whitehall. *See also* Palladian.

**corbel** Projecting bracket in a wall supporting a vault or beam.

**cornice** Part of the entablature (upper part) of a classical order, consisting of a moulded decoration set horizontally above the frieze. Also (more generally) the moulding between wall and ceiling.

**course** Continuous line or layer of stones or bricks in a wall.

**cupola** Dome.

**curtain wall** A castle's outer wall, linking its towers.

**drawbridge** Movable bridge across the castle moat. Drawbridges could be moved horizontally or lifted vertically.

**dressed stone** Trimmed, smoothed and neatly cut stone.

**eave** Part of a sloping roof that projects over the top of the wall.

**English bond** In brickwork, the alternating use along a course of the brick ends ('headers') and the brick sides ('stretchers'). *See also* Flemish bond.

**entablature** The part of the classical order that is above a wall or column. Includes the architrave, the frieze and the cornice.

**façade** One of the main exteriors of a building, usually containing an entrance.

**facing** Layer of one material laid over another.

**Flemish bond** In brickwork, the use of the brick ends ('headers') throughout one course and then the brick sides ('stretchers') throughout the next. *See also* English bond.

**fluting** Vertical series of grooves cut on classical columns etc. *See also* orders.

**frieze** Part of the entablature of a classical order, found above the architrave and consisting of decorative sculpted or painted decoration. Also used more generally for a continuous strip of decoration around the upper walls of a room.

**gable** Triangular profile at the end of a gable-roof (one with two sloping sides). Sometimes, also, a triangular extension above a doorway.

**garderobe** In castles and medieval houses, a privy or toilet. Alternatively, a walk-in wardrobe.

**Gothic** Series of styles in medieval architecture *c.*1150–*c.*1500. In England, it applied principally to ecclesiastical architecture: there were no castles or fortified manor houses built in the Gothic style.

**Great Hall** Main room in the castle or medieval house, used up to Tudor times for dining and social occasions.

**ha-ha** Sunken ditch creating a hidden boundary between gardens and parkland in a country estate. Invented in the 18th century, it was invisible from the house and was reputedly named after the expression of surprise ('Ha! Ha!') uttered when a visitor chanced upon it. It kept grazing parkland animals out of the gardens.

**hammer-beam roof** One in which the roof arch is supported by short beams set into the wall at the base of the roof.

**keep** Most strongly fortified part of a castle, usually containing the lord's apartments and often called the *donjon* (French for 'lordship'). It functioned as a stronghold within the castle to which defenders could retreat if the outer bailey were captured by besiegers. The keep was usually a stone tower standing on the motte, when there was one.

**linen-fold panelling** Tudor decorative carving of wood, which was made to look like folded linen. An example is the linen-fold panelling screen in the Great Hall at Compton Wynyates.

**Long Gallery** Feature of Tudor and especially Elizabethan-Jacobean houses, a long room was used as a promenade in bad weather and to display portraits and sculptures. There are fine examples at Hardwick Hall and Montacute.

**machicolation** Section projecting from the outer face of a castle's curtain wall, with holes in the floor through which the defenders dropped missiles. Strictly, the machicolations were the actual holes.

**mathematical tiles** Tiles that resemble brick or stone. Used, for example, by Henry Holland to reface Althorp *c.*1790. Brick taxes around this time boosted the popularity of tiles as an alternative to bricks.

**moat** Man-made ditch surrounding a castle or town walls, usually full of water.

**motte** Mound on which the keep of a castle was built. *See also* bailey.

**mullion** Vertical divider in a window containing more than one pane of glass (light). *See also* transom.

**obelisk** Tall square column tapering to a pyramidal tip. Obelisks were often raised among temples and other garden buildings in the carefully planned parklands of Baroque and Palladian houses.

**orders** Column types in ancient Greek and Roman architecture, used in classical, Palladian and Greek Revival English buildings. There are five types: the plain and unornamented Tuscan; Doric, which has triglyphs (channelled blocks) along the frieze; Ionic, which has decoration like a scroll of parchment in the capital (the head of the column); Corinthian, which has decoration representing acanthus leaves on the capital; and Composite, which combines scroll and leaf decoration.

**oriel window** Projecting window supported by stone brackets or corbels.

**Palladian** 18th-century development of the classical style in architecture, named after and inspired by the works of the great Italian Renaissance architect Andrea Palladio (1508–80). Holkham Hall and Mereworth Castle are good examples of Palladian country houses.

**pediment** Raised triangular feature above a portico, door or window. It derived from the triangular gable ends of Greek temples with pitched roofs.

*piano nobile* Derived from the Italian *palazzo*, the first-floor level containing the main rooms in a classical building.

**pilaster** Flattened column used for decorative effect on a façade. A pilaster follows the rules of the classical orders. It has no structural function.

**portcullis** Grill of wood or iron lowered for added defensive strength over a castle gateway.

**portico** Porch with roof and often pediment supported by columns.

*Left: St George's Hall, Windsor Castle.*

*Above: Nottingham Castle.*

**postern** Small, secondary gate (often concealed) in castle or town walls. Members of the garrison could use the postern to make inconspicuous exits and entries or to launch a surprise attack on a besieging force.

**revetment** Retaining wall of masonry etc supporting the face of an earthen rampart or ditch.

**Revival** Use by patrons and architects of elements from an earlier architectural style. Examples include the late 18th-century/early 19th-century Greek Revival, and the several allied Victorian movements, such as the Norman, Tudor, Elizabethan and 'Jacobethan' Revivals.

**rusticated** Stone blocks that have been dressed roughly to suggest strength.

**scroll** Decorative moulding in the shape of an S.

**shingles** Wood pieces used in place of tiles.

**solar** Private chamber, usually on the first floor of a medieval–Tudor house, to which the lord's family could retreat from the public space of the Great Hall. The solar was so called because it was fitted with large windows to allow in as much sunlight as possible.

**spandrel** Triangular space between an arch and a wall or between two arches.

**squints** hidden openings in a wall.

**strapwork** Late 16th- and early 17th-century style in ornament, making use of interlaced leather-like bands.

**transom** Horizontal divider in a window containing more than one pane of glass (light). *See also* mullion.

# PROPERTY LISTINGS

All information was accurate at the time of going to press.

**AUDLEY END HOUSE**
Saffron Walden
Essex
CB11 4JF
01799 522399
www.english-heritage.org.uk

**BALFOUR CASTLE**
Lisnaskea
Fermanagh
BT92 0JE
028 6632 3110
www.discovernorthernireland.com

**BANQUETING HOUSE, THE**
Whitehall
London
SW1A 2ER
0870 751 5178
www.hrp.org.uk/BanquetingHouse

Beaulieu
Brockenhurst
Hampshire
SO42 7ZN
01590 612345
www.beaulieu.co.uk

**BELTON HOUSE**
Grantham
Lincolnshire
NG32 2LS
01476 566116
www.nationaltrust.org.uk

**BLICKLING HALL**
Norwich
Norfolk
NR11 6NF
01263 738030
www.nationaltrust.org.uk

**BOLSOVER CASTLE**
Bolsover, Chesterfield
Derbyshire
S44 6PR
01246 822844
www.english-heritage.org.uk

**BOUGHTON HOUSE**
Kettering
Northamptonshire
NN14 1BJ
01536 515731
www.boughtonhouse.org.uk

**BURGHLEY HOUSE**
Stamford, Lincolnshire
PE9 3JY
01780 752451
www.burghley.co.uk

**CAREW CASTLE**
Tenby, Pembrokeshire
SE70 8SL
01646 651782
www.carewcastle.com

**CASTLE HOWARD**
York,
North Yorkshire
YO60 7DA
01653 648 444
www.castlehoward.co.uk

**CHATSWORTH**
Bakewell
Derbyshire
DE45 1PP
01246 565300
www.chatsworth.org

*Left: Ingatestone Hall.*

*Above: Wakehurst Place.*

**CRAIGIEVAR CASTLE**
Alford
Aberdeen and Grampian
AB33 8JF
0844 4932174
www.nts.org.uk

**CRATHES CASTLE**
Banchory
Aberdeen and Grampian
AB31 5QJ
0844 4932166
www.nts.org.uk

**DEAL CASTLE**
Deal
Kent
CT14 7BA
01304 372762
www.english-heritage.org.uk

**DELGATIE CASTLE**
Turriff
Aberdeenshire
AB53 5TD
01888 563479
www.delgatiecastle.com

**DUNFERMLINE ABBEY AND PALACE**
Dunfermline
Fife
KY12 7PD
01383 739026
www.historic-scotland.gov.uk

**DUNLUCE CASTLE**
Bushmills
County Antrim
BT57 8UY
028 207 31938
www.northantrim.com/dunlucecastle.htm

**EDINBURGH CASTLE**
Castlehill
Edinburgh
EH12NG
0131 225 9846
www.edinburghcastle.gov.uk

**ELTHAM PALACE**
Greenwich
SE9 5QE
020 8294 2548
www.elthampalace.org.uk

**ENNISKILLEN CASTLE**
Enniskillen
Co Fermanagh
BT74 7HL
028 66 325 000
www.enniskillencastle.co.uk

**FALKLAND PALACE**
Falkland
Cupar
Fife
KY15 7BU
0844 493 2186
www.nts.org.uk

**FELBRIGG HALL**
Norwich
Norfolk
NR11 8PR
01263 837444
www.nationaltrust.org.uk

**GLAMIS CASTLE**
Glamis
Angus
DD8 1RJ
01307 840393
www.glamis-castle.co.uk

**HAMPTON COURT PALACE**
East Molesey, Surrey
KT8 9AU
0870 752 7777
www.hrp.org.uk/hamptoncourtpalace

**HARDWICK HALL**
Doe Lea
Chesterfield
Derbyshire
S44 5QJ
01246 850430
www.nationaltrust.org.uk

**HATFIELD HOUSE**
Hatfield
Hertfordshire
AL9 5NQ
01707 287010
www.hatfield-house.co.uk

**HEVER CASTLE**
Hever
Edenbridge
Kent
TN8 7NG
01732 865224
www.hever-castle.co.uk

**HOLDENBY HOUSE**
Northampton
Northamptonshire
NN6 8DJ
01604 770 074
www.holdenby.com

**HOLYROODHOUSE PALACE**
Canongate
The Royal Mile
Edinburgh
EH8 8DX
0131 556 5100
www.royalcollection.org.uk

*Left: Kenilworth Castle.*

*Above: Leith Hall.*

**INGATESTONE HALL**
Ingatestone
Brentwood
Essex
CM4 9NR
01277 353010
www.enjoyengland.com

**KENILWORTH CASTLE**
Kenilworth
Warwickshire
CV8 1NE
01926 852078
www.english-heritage.org.uk

**KENSINGTON PALACE**
Kensington Gardens
London
W8 4PX
0844 482 7777
www.hrp.org.uk/KensingtonPalace

**KINGSTON LACEY**
Wimborne Minster
Dorset
BH21 4EA
01202 883402
www.nationaltrust.org.uk

**KNOLE**
Sevenoaks, Kent
TN15 0RP
01732 462100
www.nationaltrust.org.uk

*Above: Monea Castle, an imposing stronghold showing Scottish influence.*

**LAUGHARNE CASTLE**
Laugharne
Carmarthenshire
SA33 4SA
01994 427906
www.cadw.wales.gov.uk

**LEEDS CASTLE**
Broomfield, Maidstone
Kent
ME17 1PL
01622 765400
www.leeds-castle.com

**LEITH HALL**
Huntly
Aberdeen and Grampian
AB54 4NQ
0844 4932175
www.nts.org.uk

**LONGLEAT HOUSE**
Longleat
Warminster
Wiltshire
BA12 7NW
01985 844400
www.longleat.co.uk

**LOSELEY PARK**
Arlington
Guildford
Surrey
GU3 1HS
01483 304440
www.loseley-park.com

**MAPLEDURHAM HOUSE**
Mapledurham
Reading
Berkshire
RG4 7TR
01189 723350
www.mapledurham.co.uk

**MARLBOROUGH HOUSE**
Pall Mall, London
SW1Y 5HX
020 7747 6491
www.thecommonwealth.org/mhouse
/index.html

**MONEA CASTLE**
Enniskillen
Fermanagh
028 66 323 110
www.discovernorthernireland.com

**MONTACUTE HOUSE**
Montacute
Somserset
TA15 6XP
01935 823289
www.nationaltrust.org.uk

**NOTTINGHAM CASTLE**
Castle Road
Nottingham
Nottinghamshire
NG1 6EL
0115 915 3700
www.nottinghamcity.gov.uk/sitemap/leisu
re_and_culture/museumsandgalleries/nott
inghamcastle.htm

**PENDENNIS CASTLE**
Falmouth, Cornwall
TR11 4LP
01326 316594
www.english-heritage.org.uk

**PETWORTH HOUSE**
Petworth
West Sussex
GU28 0AE
01798 342207
www.nationaltrust.org.uk

*Right: Hampton Court Palace.*

**POWIS CASTLE**
Welshpool, Powys
SY21 8RF
01938 551929
www.nationaltrust.org.uk

**QUEEN'S HOUSE**
Park Row, Greenwich
London
SE10 9NF
020 8858 4422
www.nmm.ac.uk

**ROTHESAY CASTLE**
Rothesay, Isle of Bute
Argyll and Bute
PA20 0DA
01700 502 691
www.historic-scotland.gov.uk

**STIRLING CASTLE**
Stirling, Stirlingshire
FK8 1EJ
01786 450 000
www.historic-scotland.gov.uk

**ST MAWES CASTLE**
St Mawes
Truro
Cornwall
TR2 5DE
01326 270526
www.english-heritage.org.uk

**STOKE PARK PAVILIONS**
Stoke Buerne
Towcester
Northamptonshire
NN12 7RZ
01604 862172

*Above: The east front, Hampton Court Palace.*

## ST PAUL'S CATHEDRAL
St Paul's Churchyard
London
EC4M 8AD
020 7246 8348
www.stpauls.co.uk

## SUDELEY CASTLE
Winchcombe
Gloucestershire
GL54 5JD
01242 602308
or 01242 604244
www.sudeleycastle.co.uk

## SULGRAVE MANOR
Sulgrave
Banbury
Oxfordshire
OX17 2SD
01295 760205
www.sulgravemanor.org.uk

## SYON HOUSE
Brentford
Middlesex
TW8 8JF
020 8560 0882
www.syonpark.co.uk

## TOWER OF LONDON
Tower Hill
London
EC3N 4AB
0870 756 6060
or 0844 482 7777
www.hrp.org.uk/toweroflondon

## TULLY CASTLE
Derrygonnelly
Fermanagh
028 90 546 552
www.ni-environment.gov.uk/tully.htm

## UPPARK
South Harting
Petersfield
West Sussex
GU31 5QR
01730 825415
www.nationaltrust.org.uk

## THE VYNE
Sherborne St John
Basingstoke
Hampshire
RG24 9HL
01256 883858
www.nationaltrust.org.uk

## WAKEHURST PLACE
Ardingly
West Sussex
RH17 6TN
01444 894000
www.nationaltrust.org.uk

## WALMER CASTLE
Walmer
Deal
Kent
CT14 7LJ
01304 364288
www.english-heritage.org.uk

## WESTON PARK
Weston-under-Lizard
Shifnal
Shropshire
TF11 8LE
01952 852100
www.weston-park.com

## WILTON HOUSE
Wilton
Salisbury
Wiltshire
SP2 0BJ
01722 746714
www.wiltonhouse.com

*Above: Marlborough House.*

## WINDSOR CASTLE
Windsor
Berkshire
SL4 1NJ
020 7766 7304
www.windsor.gov.uk or
www.royalcollection.org.uk

## WOLLATON HALL
Wollaton
Nottingham
Nottinghamshire
NG8 2AE
0115 9153911
http://www.nottinghamcity.gov.uk/
sitemap/leisure_and_culture/museums
andgalleries/wollatonhall.htm

*Below: Delgatie Castle, rebuilt in the 16th century in the Scottish Baronial style.*

# INDEX

**Alamy**: Arcaid: 63br; Jon Arnold Images: 28br; Roger Bamber: 87tr; Quentin Bargate: 60t; Bildarchiv Monheim GmbH: 31b, 32; Michael Booth: 52-3; G P Bowater: 41b; Adrian Chinery: 62; David Copeman: 65b; CW Images: 13tr, 48t; Detail Nottingham: 51tc; EDIFICE: 43b; Elmtree Images: 6–7; Europhotos: 55t; Mary Evans Picture Library: 18b, 24, 40cr; eye35.com: 9t, 28bl, 74b; Paul Felix Photography: 46br; Joe Fox: 13c, 69t; Alan Gallery: 68t; Tim Graham: 83br; Robert Harding Picture Library Ltd: 16–17; Mike Haywood: 81tr; Jeremy Hoare: 63t; The Hoberman Collection: 83bl; Michael Jenner: 29t, 67b; Justin Kase: 10tc, 34–5, 43t; Pawel Libera: 21t; David Lyons: 49b; Neil McAllister: 46t; Jeff Morgan: 49t; nagelstock.com: 29b, 42b, 45b; Frank Naylor: 58; North Wind Pictures Archives: 79t; David Norton Photography: 75b; Peter Packer: 37b, 37t; Photofrenetic: 25tl; Pictorial Press Ltd: 87br; Popperfoto: 27bl, 85b; Powered by Light/Alan Spencer: 33c; Purestock: 59b; Rob Rayworth: 89; Nigel Reed: 31t; Rolf Richardson: 39b; David Sanger Photography: 59t; Brian Seed: 21c, 61t; Simmons Aerofilms Ltd: 57t; Skyscan Photolibrary: 30b, 38, 45t, 66t; Nigel Stollery: 76t; Worldwide Picture Library: 40bl

*Below: A pond garden at Hampton Court.*

*Above: Kingston Lacy.*

**The Art Archive**: 66b; Jarrold Publishing: 2, 8b, 21b, 61br, 69bl; Palazzo Barberini Rome/Dagli Orti: 30t; Neil Setchfield: 12; Victoria & Albert Museum London/Eileen Tweedy: 20b; John Webb: 64t

**The Bridgeman Archive**: John Bethell/ Audley End, Essex: 60b; Compton Wynyates, Warwickshire: 18t; Hardwick Hall, Derbyshire: 44t; Hatfield House, Hertfordshire: 56b; Knole House, Sevenoaks, Kent: 55b, 54b; © Collection of the Earl of Pembroke, Wilton House, Wilts: 67t; © Collection of the New-York Historical Society: 26t; Corning Museum of Glass, New York: 27t; Crathes Castle, Kincardineshire: 41t; Mark Fiennes, Hatfield House, Hertfordshire: 56t; Hever Castle Ltd, Kent: 22tr; © Mallett Gallery, London: Private Collection: 51b; Marlborough House, London: 63bl; Montacute House, Somerset: 51tl; National Portrait Gallery, London: 36t; National Trust Photographic Library/John Hammond, Hardwick Hall, Derbyshire: 44b; Petworth House, Sussex: 72b; Private Collection: 54t, 65t; © The Royal Cornwall Museum, Truro, Cornwall: 39t; Syon House, Middlesex: 74t; The Stapleton Collection, Private Collection: 25tr, 64b, 83t, 72t; Topham Picturepoint, Compton Wynyates, Warwickshire: 19t/Petworth House, West Sussex: 73b; Ken Welsh/Private Collection: 81b

**Carew Castle**: 48bl, 48br

**Corbis**: Peter Aprahamian: 87bl; Chris Bland/Eye Ubiquitous: 50b; Mike Finn-Kelcey/ Reuters: 85t; Hulton-Deutsch Collection: 46bl; Clay Perry: 78b

**Ynys Crowston-Boaler**: 5r, 79b, 89tr, 96br

**John Clare**: 4c, 4r, 5l, 5c, 90bl, 90tr, 91tr, 93br, 96t

**Mary Evans Picture Library**: 84t

**Leeds Castle**: 23t, 23b

**Loseley Park**: 47b, 47tc, 47tr

**Pictures of Britain**: Jeffrey Beazley: 76b; John D Beldom: 80b; John Blake: 9b, 19b; Mike Cowen: 81t; Brian Gadsby: 28t; Brian Gibbs: 25b; Ron Gregory: 33b, 78t; Antony Hebdon: 73t; Paul I Makepeace: 26b, 27br; John Mole: 33t; Chris Parker: 22t; John Tremaine: 61bl; Jeffery Whitelaw: 50t; Julian Worker: 36b

**Rex Features**: BNP/NAP: 42t; Chris Capstick: 22bl; Simon Roberts: 86b; The Travel Library: 70-1, 77; John Winders: 57b

**Joy Wotton**: 1, 3, 4l, 8t, 10tl, 10tr, 20tc, 20tr, 82b, 82tc, 82tr, 84b, 86t, 88, 92br, 93tl and tr, 96bl

*Below: Nottingham Castle.*